Community Care

Neil Thompson
and
Sue Thompson

TiP Theory into Practice
Series Editor Neil Thompson

RHP

First published in 2005 by:
Russell House Publishing Ltd.
4 St. George's House
Uplyme Road
Lyme Regis
Dorset DT7 3LS
Tel: 01297-443948
Fax: 01297-442722
e-mail: help@russellhouse.co.uk
www.russellhouse.co.uk

© Neil Thompson and Sue Thompson

The moral right of Neil Thompson and Sue Thompson to be identified as the authors of this work has been asserted by them in accordance with The Copyright Designs and Patents Act 1988.

British Library Cataloguing-in-publication Data:

A catalogue record for this book is available from the British Library.

ISBN: 1-903855-58-6

Typeset by TW Typesetting, Plymouth, Devon
Printed by Alden, Oxford

About Russell House Publishing

RHP is a group of social work, probation, education and youth and community work practitioners and academics working in collaboration with a professional publishing team.

Our aim is to work closely with the field to produce innovative and valuable materials to help managers, trainers, practitioners and students.

We are keen to receive feedback on publications and new ideas for future projects.

For details of our other publications please visit our website or ask us for a catalogue. Contact details are on this page.

Contents

The Theory into Practice Series

This exciting new series fills a significant gap in the market for short, user-friendly texts, written by experts, that succinctly introduce sets of theoretical ideas, relate them clearly to practice issues, and guide the reader to further learning. They particularly address discrimination, oppression, equality and diversity. They can be read either as general overviews of particular areas of theory and practice, or as foundations for further study. The series will be invaluable across the human services, including social work and social care; youth and community work; criminal and community justice work; counselling; advice work; housing; and aspects of health care.

About the Series Editor

Neil Thompson is a Director of Avenue Consulting Ltd (www.avenueconsulting.co.uk), a company offering training and consultancy in relation to social work and human relations issues. He was formerly Professor of Applied Social Studies at Staffordshire University. He has over 100 publications to his name, including best-selling textbooks, papers in scholarly journals and training and open learning materials.

Neil is a Fellow of the Chartered Institute of Personnel and Development, the Institute of Training and Occupational Learning and the Royal Society of Arts (elected on the basis of his contribution to organisational learning). He is the editor of the *British Journal of Occupational Learning* (wwwtraininginstitute.co.uk). He was also responsible for the setting up of the self-help website, www.humansolutions.org.uk. His personal website is at www.neilthompson.info.

Prospective authors wishing to make a contribution to the *Theory into Practice* series should contact Neil via his company website, www.avenueconsulting.co.uk.

Series Editor's Foreword

About the series

The relationship between theory and practice is one that has puzzled practitioners and theorists alike for some considerable time, and there still remains considerable debate about how the two interconnect. However, what is clear is that it is dangerous to tackle the complex problems encountered in 'people work' without having at least a basic understanding of what makes people tick, of how the social context plays a part in both the problems we address and the solutions we seek. Working with people and their problems is difficult and demanding work. To try to undertake it without being armed with a sound professional knowledge base is a very risky strategy indeed, and potentially a disastrous one.

An approach to practice based mainly on guesswork, untested assumptions, habit and copying others is clearly not one that can be supported. Good practice must be an *informed* practice, with actions based, as far as possible, on reasoning, understanding and evidence. This series is intended to develop just such good practice by providing:

- an introductory overview of a particular area of theory or professional knowledge;
- an exploration of how it relates to practice issues;
- a consideration of how the theory base can help tackle discrimination and oppression; and
- a guide to further learning.

The texts in the series are written by people with extensive knowledge and practical experience in the fields concerned and are intended as an introduction to the wider and more in-depth literature base.

About this book

This particular text, with its focus on community care, offers a clear account of some of the key issues underpinning understanding of practice. It argues strongly against forms of community care practice that are mechanistic and simplistic in their approach to meeting vulnerable people's needs. In place of such a dangerous and dehumanising approach, the authors argue the case for an informed approach that places people at the heart of the undertaking.

The community care reforms in the early part of the 1990s brought about significant changes in how community care issues are managed and practised, but perhaps with mixed results. That is, while some improvements can be identified, there have also been concerns that the system leaves a great deal to be desired. This book will not make up for the inadequacies of the system, but it will help to lay the foundations for good practice in this important area of personal social services.

Neil Thompson, Series Editor

About the authors

Neil and **Sue Thompson** are both Directors of Avenue Consulting Ltd (www.avenueconsulting.co.uk), a company offering training and consultancy in relation to such problems as discrimination, stress, conflict, bullying and harassment and loss, grief and trauma. They have co-written *Understanding Social Care* (Russell House Publishing, 2002). They have also collaborated on developing the self-help website, www.humansolutions.org.uk.

Neil was formerly Professor of Applied Social Studies at Staffordshire University. He has over 100 publications to his name, including best-selling textbooks, such as *People Skills* (Palgrave Macmillan, 2nd edn, 2002). He is the editor of the *British Journal of Occupational Learning.* His website is at www.neilthompson.info.

Sue has extensive experience in the caring professions as a nurse, care manager and social worker. She is the author of *From Where I'm Sitting*, a training manual on work with older people (Russell House Publishing, 2002) and *Age Discrimination* (Russell House Publishing, 2005), as well as a number of book chapters and articles. She also tutors on an Open University undergraduate course which explores the concepts of care, welfare and community.

Introduction

'Community care' is a term that means different things to different people. For example, the periodical entitled *Community Care* covers a wide range of issues relating to social work and social care. However, the sense in which we use the terms here is that of the various efforts to help ensure that people who are in need of care are helped to remain in the community, avoiding the need for institutional care.

We focus a great deal on the process of care management, with its emphasis on assessing needs and developing a package of care services and other measures to solve problems and promote independence. This is seen in the broader legal and policy context which puts community care at the forefront of social services for potentially vulnerable groups, such as older or disabled people, people with mental health problems or learning disabilities and so on.

Community care is not a panacea, but in promoting the benefits of a strong focus on community provision, we must bear in mind the costs (more in human terms than financial) of a reliance on institutional care.

The book is divided into four main parts. Part One provides an introductory overview of the theory base underpinning community care practice. It is by no means an exhaustive account, but it should be sufficient to lay the foundations for future learning and development. Part Two builds on that foundation by exploring a range of practice issues. Part Three addresses issues of discrimination and oppression to try to ensure that practice is based on principles of equality and social justice. Part Four acts as a guide to further learning, providing guidance on additional reading plus details of relevant organisations and websites.

We hope you will find the book of value and will benefit from what it has to offer. In particular, we hope you will use it as a gateway to the extensive literature base in order to make the most of the learning opportunities available to you.

Notes

1. The terms used to refer to recipients of community care are contested ones, with no single agreed term. Perhaps the most common these days is 'service user' but some people object to this term. Our preferred term is 'client', although we recognise that some people feel that this term has elitist connotations. In our view, client is the term that best fits our model of community care practice as professional practice. However, we do use alternative terms from time to time, simply for the sake of stylistic variety.
2. At various points in the text you will find exercises. While you may be tempted to skip these and simply continue reading the main text, we would strongly

recommend that you do spend some time addressing the issues raised by the exercises as this should help you to deepen your understanding and to link theory and practice.

Introduction

Our aim in Part One is to present some of the basic elements of the underpinning 'theory' or knowledge base relating to community care, although it has to be recognised that, in the space available, we can realistically provide only a selective account of what amounts to a very large and complex knowledge base. It is therefore important to recognise that the ideas presented here are intended as an introduction to the wider literature relating to the knowledge base rather than as an alternative to that literature (see Part Four for detailed guidance on further reading).

In this part of the book we present some important issues for you to consider in order to help you develop a good understanding of the nature of community care and its importance. In order to do this we have divided Part One into three chapters. Chapter 1, *Understanding Community Care*, concentrates on care management, a central plank in community care practice, and seeks to establish what it is (and what it is not); explores some of the complexities of risk management; clarifies what is involved in empowerment; and examines the emergence of evidence-based practice as an important, if contested, dimension of good practice.

Chapter 2 has as its topic the broad field of law and regulation. Here we examine the legal basis of community care and how professional practice is monitored and regulated. Chapter 3 explores the important concept of partnership and sets the scene for a more detailed discussion in Part Two of the three different levels of partnership working: with clients, with carers and with staff from other agencies.

Each of the three chapters ends with a set of 'Points to Ponder', questions to help you relate the theoretical ideas presented to your own work and circumstances.

Chapter 1
Understanding Community Care

The Centre for Policy on Ageing offer a useful starting point when it comes to understanding community care:

> The term 'community care' is here used to describe that network of care which will maintain people or, where necessary, restore people to independent living. Customarily, this will be achieved by enabling them to live normally in their own homes. (1990, p. 16)

For a very long time the dominant way of dealing with certain groups of people was to remove them from society and place them in an institution. For example, people with mental health problems or learning disabilities were placed in hospitals away from mainstream society – 'out of sight, out of mind', as it were. The philosophy underpinning this approach was based on the idea that it was safest for both those institutionalised and for society at large if they were kept separate.

In recent decades we have adopted a different approach, one in which the detrimental effects of institutionalisation have been recognised. Over time policy makers have come to realise that integrating people into the community is a more humane way of dealing with issues relating to mental health and disability. Thus the era of community care was born, an era in which great efforts have been made to replace large-scale institutions with a range of services geared towards maintaining people in the community as far as possible. How those services work is a major theme of this book.

This ethos of community care has meant a major change in how social policy is managed and practised. It has led to significant changes in society's treatment of certain groups who were previously excluded from the mainstream of society. Seed and Kaye (1994) point out that the philosophy underpinning community care encompasses the following four elements:

1. *'Quality of life'*. Quality of life criteria should be adopted for assessing people's needs for support in personal care and daily living in the community. 'Quality of life' includes material, social and spiritual well-being in a safe environment.
2. *Individualisation*. An integrated and individualised response to assessed needs on the part of the health and social services.
3. *Participation*. A participatory approach to the provision of services, emphasising personal choice.

4. *Developing potential.* Building on existing or potential sources of support from relatives, friends, neighbourhood resources and other components of people's social networks. (p. 5)

This passage raises some important points, chiefly the following:

- *Spiritual well-being.* A common criticism of some forms of care management is that they tend to focus almost exclusively on practical needs without paying attention to wider or deeper needs relating to emotional or spiritual matters. It can be argued that a failure to address such needs will, in the long run, necessitate greater expenditure on practical needs and will create dependency rather than contribute to empowerment. See the discussion of loss below. See also Coleman *et al.* (2002) for a discussion of the important role of spirituality in relation to older people's abilities to adjust to the loss of a spouse.

- *Individualisation.* The need to be clear that clients are unique individuals and not simply members of categories is, of course, a basic and long-standing part of the value base underpinning the provision of personal social services. As Orme and Glastonbury (1993) comment: 'It is about matching flexible services to identified needs rather than fitting people into inflexible services' (p. 4). Services are likely to be of little use if they are applied on a blanket basis rather than tailored to the specific needs of the individual concerned. However, while certainly upholding the value of individualisation, we would also want to draw attention to the other side of the coin, namely what Thompson *et al.* (1994) refer to as 'deindividualisation'. This involves recognising that individuals are also part of wider social networks and structural patterns, and that we should not neglect these wider considerations if we are to offer an anti-discriminatory service. Every one of us is indeed a unique individual in our own right, but we are also unique individuals in a social context. This is a point to which we shall return in Part Three.

- *User involvement.* Beresford (2001) argues that social policy has been slow to take up the challenge of making user involvement a reality and urges us to move beyond the rhetoric. Indeed, community care in general and care management in particular provide important opportunities for developing genuine partnerships and moving away from traditional notions of 'the expert knows best'. The client's input into the care management process is often crucial in making it a success. Without their full acceptance of and commitment to what is being done, it is unlikely that they will gain full advantage from the resources being deployed. Partnership and involvement are therefore not just abstract ethical principles, but also very concrete elements of good practice (see Chapter 3).

- *Networking.* The ability to draw upon wider networks of support and resources is clearly crucial in a world in which demand exceeds supply and available resources are therefore likely to be oversubscribed on a regular basis. This is a skilled area of practice and it is not enough simply to urge practitioners to undertake these roles without first considering what is involved and how the appropriate knowledge, skills and values can be developed over time. It is for this reason that networking, as part of multidisciplinary collaboration, is discussed in more detail in Part Two.

The first of these four points is particularly significant, as the care management approach (which we shall discuss below) has been criticised for allowing mechanistic approaches to squeeze out issues of emotional support (Hoyes *et al.*, 1994). Similarly, criticisms have been made of mechanistic approaches which run counter to the principle of needs-led assessment. As Phillips (1996) points out:

> the tendency to a service-led approach appears to have been unintentionally condoned by the development of lengthy, check-list type assessment forms (Petch *et al.*, 1994; Caldock and Nolan, 1994).
>
> Literature has also recently emerged critiquing the process of assessment and in particular the paperwork surrounding it, highlighting the length and inflexibility of the forms (Petch *et al.*, 1994). A survey of 65 practitioners in Scotland found that forms seemed to become ends in themselves and also tended to disempower clients (MacDonald and Myers, 1995). The fear expressed by social workers is that assessment will become a mechanical, bureaucratic process rather than serving client need. (p. 9)

What is care management?

Care management is the term used to refer to the role that has developed from the policy changes in care provision which established an emphasis on providing care to vulnerable people in their own homes and communities, rather than in centralised and institutionalised environments. That is, care management is part of the philosophy, policy and practice of community care.

Inherent in care management is an emphasis on providing and managing individualised packages of care, tailored as far as possible to individual need, rather than offering a 'one size fits all' provision which may or may not meet everyone's circumstances or pocket. To continue the tailoring analogy, care management is about buying the cloth, buttons and thread in order to make a jacket that will fit the person you have measured and agreed the style with, rather than sending him or her along to the nearest department store to collect an off-the-peg garment which will serve the purpose to some extent, perhaps, but neither fit properly nor take account of individual preference or circumstance.

An important underpinning principle is that of 'needs-led assessment', a widely used, but unfortunately often misunderstood, concept. It refers to the importance of ensuring that assessment processes identify people's needs and the problems that need to be solved to meet those needs. It is intended as a replacement for the traditional service-led approach where the focus is on simply matching up individual needs and existing services. Of course, the problem with a service-led approach is that it blocks i) the identification of unmet need to feed into the policy review and development process (if assessment is geared towards existing services only, unmet need will not be considered); and ii) the development of creative approaches (if services are not available to meet identified need, then creative problem solving becomes an important set of skills to develop).

Another important aspect of assessment is the need to determine the appropriate level of assessment. Many people will require only a very basic level of service, while others will have very complex needs, and so it is important that assessment processes are sufficiently sophisticated to identify which cases require which level of input. It is the latter group, those with complex needs, who will become the users of care management services.

Phillips (1996) lists the core functions of care management as follows:

- providing information about available assistance
- determining the level of assessment
- the assessing of need
- producing care plans
- securing the necessary resources and services to implement the plans
- monitoring the arrangements
- reviewing the user's needs (p. 6)

These are clearly tasks that are entirely consistent with traditional social work. We would hope, then, that you can appreciate that care management can be seen as a *branch* of social work which, admittedly, is different in some ways from other forms of social work. But it *is* social work, not an abandonment of it. This is a point to which we shall return below.

While the National Health Service and Community Care Act 1990 has had a big impact on the way social care services were organised and delivered, bringing the concept of care management and its implications to the fore, community care itself had been a feature of social policy debate for some two decades before the emergence of the Act (Phillips, 1996). With the Act itself came an obligation for local authorities to develop strategies for purchasing rather than providing care, and with that strategic development came the development of procedures and working practices for individual workers. The care management model requires individual workers to act as brokers – to use their skills to put together a package of care from a variety of sources, including private, voluntary and public sector provision and, of course, the informal support of family, neighbours and friends.

This is, in fact, not too far removed from what social workers had been doing before the implementation of the Act – that is to say, drawing on a 'patchwork' of services or support to respond to identified need. What c. significantly, perhaps, was the onus on care managers to manag. responses within a prescribed budget. It is this additional role which is seen many care managers as a major and often unwelcome change to the nature of the work they do in terms of increased paperwork and less face-to-face contact (Jones, 2001; Postle, 2002) and leads many to argue that what they are doing is not social work. If you feel like this, we would ask that you step back for a moment and consider whether or not you regard the skills you use (assessing, negotiating, prioritising and so on) as social work skills, the values that underpin your work (treating people with dignity and respect, uniqueness of the individual, valuing equality and diversity and so on) as social work values and the tasks you perform (assessing need, working in partnership to meet need, encouraging service users to call on their own resources to promote change) as social work tasks.

Managing risk

Of course, no situation we enter in life is free from risk. What we need to consider, then, is not how we avoid risks – as that would clearly be unrealistic – but, rather, how to assess risks and manage them as effectively as possible.

Risk is a very complex issue, with a large and growing literature base. Our discussions here must therefore be seen as introductory rather than exhaustive. The points we raise here are intended to provide an overview of the subject so that you can begin to understand the complexities involved. Suggestions for further reading on the subject are to be found in Part Four.

An important point to be emphasised is that the assessment component of the care manager role is not simply about assessing needs, as this would be far too narrow a focus and would leave both worker and client in some difficulty in certain circumstances where the level of risk is worryingly high. An understanding of risk and how to assess it is therefore a fundamental part of the knowledge repertoire a care manager needs. We would like to propose the following points as key issues that need to be taken into account:

- *Risk of what?* It is important to be clear about what danger we are seeking to avoid. It is necessary to focus quite specifically, rather than rely on a vague notion of being 'at risk'. If we are not precise about what specific dangers a person faces we will find it difficult if not impossible to develop a plan of action for addressing these dangers.
- *The balance of risks.* It is, of course, a gross oversimplification to regard risk management as the pursuit of a risk-free situation. All situations involve some degree of risk, and so what has to be recognised is that pursuing a course of action with a view to reducing or removing particular risks is likely to involve introducing new risks. For example, admission to residential care may

remove some of the risks of living alone in the community but will introduce the risks of living in a communal environment – including the potentially very harmful psychological effects of giving up one's own home (Peace *et al.*, 1997, p. 43; S. Thompson, 2002a).

- *Risks and rights*. Risk management is not simply a matter of dealing with risks as hazards to be avoided or minimised. We also need to recognise that risks have to be balanced against rights. For example, if a person (of sound mind) chooses to live with risks which others find unacceptable, we cannot assume that we are in a position to act against the wishes of the client. Situations which involve a conflict between an individual's right to self-determination and perceived risk can be very difficult to manage and require considerable sensitivity.
- *Risk and identity*. It should also be borne in mind that our sense of self often owes much to the risks that we take. For example, work roles, hobbies and relationships all involve some degree of risk. If we were to be 'wrapped up in cotton wool' and prevented from taking risks, our self-esteem would be likely to be undermined and our sense of identity compromised. This can have major consequences in terms of motivation, in some circumstances leading to depression; and can also bring about frustration, perhaps leading to violence and/or aggression.

In addition to these points we feel it is important to stress the point made above that risk assessment is (or at least should be) part and parcel of the broader process of assessment, rather than something that is only undertaken in what are perceived as high-risk situations. To reserve risk assessment for such occasions means that we are likely to miss out on the important task of dealing with risk issues before they intensify and perhaps become too problematic. It is important to maintain a balance between adopting a panic response to risk (which has unfortunately been far too common in some settings) on the one hand, and being complacent on the other.

Practice Focus 1.1

Maria was asked to visit Andrea to undertake an assessment of need. Andrea was a 28-year-old woman with learning difficulties, living at home with the support of her father, who worked away from home during the day. Although her father left a ready-prepared lunch for her, Andrea often tried to use the gas cooker, which had resulted in several serious fires. Maria's first impression was that Andrea's judgement was impaired and that she needed constant supervision and guidance. She thought about arranging for her to attend a day centre, or talking to her father about the feasibility of his continuing to work full-time. However, after undertaking an assessment of risk, she was able to clarify that the cooking posed the only risk.

This led to a re-evaluation of her initial response and, with the fitting of a disabling device to the cooker and a phone call from her father to remind her where her packed lunch was, Andrea was enabled to continue living at home with her father. On reflection Maria realised how inappropriate her response might have been had she not incorporated an assessment of risk into her assessment of need.

This is the case in relation to not only risk *assessment*, but also risk *management*. Assessing the degree and nature of risks is only part of the story, of course. What is also needed is a strategy for managing those risks once they have been identified. This is clearly an important role for care managers, as the package of care that is put together must take account of any significant risk issues, as we must recognise that, underlying any set of needs identified through assessment will be a basic need for safety and freedom from harm. This underlying need is something that has long been recognised as an aspect of good practice. However, the implementation of the Human Rights Act 1998 in October 2000 has elevated this from a matter of good practice to one of legally necessary practice. This is because Article 5 of the European Convention on Human Rights guarantees individuals a 'right to liberty and security of the person'. The right to 'security of the person' means that every reasonable effort must be made to ensure that service users (and indeed carers) are as safe from harm as they realistically can be.

Empowerment

The term 'empowerment' is one that is used often in the caring professions, but not always in an uncritical way. It has been the subject of much debate and, of late, has become a 'buzzword' – one of those words that keeps cropping up in mission statements and so on, but is not necessarily well understood by those who use it. That is not to say that it is not important. Indeed, we would argue that power, and the ways in which it is handled, are crucial issues to consider.

So, what does empowerment actually mean when used in a community care context? Adams (2002) defines it as follows:

> the means by which individuals, groups and/or communities become able to take control of their circumstances and achieve their own goals, thereby being able to work towards helping themselves and others to maximise the quality of their lives. (p. 8)

To avoid oversimplification what we need to recognise is that empowerment is not a matter of 'giving people power', as if power is a simple commodity that can be handed from one person to another. Power is a complex, multilevel phenomenon, and so we need to develop a more sophisticated understanding than this 'commodity' approach if we are to do it justice (Thompson, 2003a).

We also need to recognise that it is not a matter of 'giving power away', as if reducing one's own power as a professional will somehow put service users in a greater position of power. Unfortunately, this is the way some people have interpreted the development of anti-discriminatory practice in general and empowerment in particular. It is a gross oversimplification and one that we have to be wary of. Power can be a force for positive and constructive change or it can be a source of oppression when it is unwittingly misused (for example, through carelessness, insensitivity or ignorance) or deliberately abused. The question, then, is not how we 'give' our power to others but, rather, how we use our own power to help people gain greater control over their lives.

Evidence-based practice

This is a relatively new approach to professional practice which has gained both ardent supporters and arch enemies. The basis of this development is a belief in the importance of establishing scientific evidence of the effectiveness of various forms of practice so that we can be clear about what works and what does not. Macdonald (2002) sums it up well as follows:

> The underpinning principle of evidence-based practice appears relatively uncontroversial: that when professionals intervene in people's lives they do so on the basis of the best available evidence regarding the likely consequences of that intervention. They should be as confident as it is possible to be that what they do will bring about the changes sought and will do so with the minimum of adverse consequences.
>
> Evidence-based practice denotes an approach to decision-making which is transparent, accountable and based on a consideration of current best evidence about the effects of particular interventions on the welfare of individuals, groups and communities. (p. 424)

This is an approach that has become a significant influence in health care circles and is increasingly playing a part in shaping thinking on social work, including community care.

Sheldon and Chilvers (2000) argue that the development of evidence-based practice is geared towards:

- Regular updating of social workers on what is known at an empirical level about the effectiveness of different approaches;
- Ensuring students are taught how to evaluate research findings as part of their basic professional training;
- Supervision incorporating discussion of the evidence on which interventions are based;
- Departmental meetings including reference to research and its implications;
- Ensuring access to relevant literature is available – for example, through library services;

- Personal responsibility for acquainting oneself with empirical evidence on effectiveness;
- The development of collaborative arrangements between social work agencies and academic institutions for promoting and disseminating research.

Clearly this is a major agenda but one which is already showing signs of development (for example, the establishment of the Centre for Evidence-Based Social Services (CEBSS) at the University of Exeter. It is an approach which has much to commend it in terms of its emphasis on the importance of drawing on the best available research evidence to inform our choice of method of intervention. However, it is also an approach which has been criticised for oversimplifying matters relating to the nature of research, its validity and applicability and the role of 'science' as a basis for practice (see, for example, Webb, 2001). It is beyond the scope of this book to explore this debate in detail. We will therefore limit ourselves to stating that we would support the basic view that more and better use should be made of research evidence on practice effectiveness, but we would argue that a critical approach to the whole issue of the relationship between research and practice needs to be adopted (see Thompson, 2000a).

Reference also needs to be made to the relationship between evidence-based practice and reflective practice. It is important to recognise that evidence-based practice should not be confused with a simplistic notion that 'the research' will tell us how to practise. While research evidence can certainly form an important part of the professional knowledge base underpinning practice, this does not mean that a research-driven approach can be a substitute for a reflective approach which seeks to integrate insights from both academic and practice sources (reflective practice will be discussed in Part Three). For one thing, research evidence will rarely, if ever, be so clear cut and unambiguous as to provide definitive prescriptions for practice and, for another, even if it were, there would still be contextual factors in the practice arena that would also need to be taken into account.

The major implication of evidence-based practice is that research evidence, particularly that relating specifically to practice effectiveness, has an important part to play in influencing decision making at both the individual case level and the wider policy level. We shall therefore now move on to examine two research studies, one which was undertaken in the early days of the implementation of the NHS and Community Care Act 1990, and one much more recent example.

Hoyes *et al.* (1994) describe research into the development of care management systems from which the following seven conclusions were drawn (pp. 5–6):

- *Local authorities are struggling to develop purchasing strategies in the context of severe resource constraints. Issues of choice and control for users and carers risk becoming secondary to such concerns.* This, of course, has continued to be an important issue and one that we are likely to be struggling with for some time to come. However, it is important that we should not allow the important issue of resource constraints to become all-important and lead to defeatism and cynical responses to the challenges of community care.

- *A mixed economy of social care provision is unlikely to provide an alternative to the 'set list' on offer for most users and carers, at least in the short term.* This is also a problem that we continue to struggle with. The idea of creative, problem-solving approaches has yet to establish itself as fully as it could (or, we would argue, as it should).

- *Users and carers have more choice and control over services where they pay the providers directly.* The introduction of direct payment schemes is an opportunity to build on this strength.

- *People often need emotional support and counselling as much as practical help; but lack of resources and bureaucratic, mechanistic approaches to care management risk squeezing out those less quantifiable services.* This point has been made earlier, namely the danger of neglecting emotional (and spiritual) matters. For example, Sue Thompson (2002b) argues that there are major dangers involved in failing to address the significance of loss in older people's lives.

- *Communication problems are evident throughout the care management process and give rise to a whole range of problems.* Effective communication is a central plank of working in partnership and so concerns about inadequacies in communication need to be taken very seriously (Thompson, 2003b).

- *Social services managers and individual fieldworkers give priority to the needs of carers over those of service users themselves.* This should alert us to the danger of the classic mistake in social work of forgetting who the client is.

- *Field-level staff need far more support and training if they are successfully to manage the changes expected of them in terms of attitudes, approaches and skills.* And, of course, this very book is partly a response to this finding.

Practice Focus 1.2

Kate had just returned from a conference where she had been interested to hear about new research into the benefits of supported housing. Managing the risks involved in maintaining dependent older people in the community had always been a concern of hers, and so she was interested to hear about the availability of such schemes and whether they had been evaluated in terms of the quality of life of the residents. Before attending the course she had thought of research as something divorced from the work she did as a care manager – that is to say, she saw it as the concern of academics. However, on returning to her workplace she realised that research was actually very relevant to her work and vowed to find out whether anyone had undertaken a comparative study of experiences in supported housing and residential care homes.

More recent research also raises concerns about the opportunities for care management to be the basis of high-quality co-ordination of care services and related matters. Postle (2002) reports on research relating to care managers working with older people. Her findings include the fact that:

> Care managers are, for example, trying to reconcile spending more time on paperwork and computer work with having less time for making and working within relationships with people. While their work is becoming increasingly complex, many of the processes are becoming increasingly reductionist. (p. 335)

She goes on to argue that the increase in tension is contributing to higher levels of stress and adversely affecting the quality of service provided (stress will be discussed in Part Two).

This research clearly presents major challenges for practitioners, managers and educators. The point that we find particularly worrying is the reference to an increasing reliance on 'reductionist' approaches – that is, those which oversimplify the complex realities of people's lives, their problems and their care needs and try to provide simple solutions (for example, a checklist as an *aid* to assessment can easily become the *basis* of that assessment).

These, then, are just two examples of how research can be used to illuminate practice. Research is, after all, a distillation of other people's experience presented in a form in which we can use it as a platform for learning although, as indicated earlier, we none the less need to adopt a critical approach to such research. We need to find the healthy balance between an anti-intellectual rejection of research and all matters theoretical on the one hand and an uncritical acceptance of research findings as 'the answer' on the other. This balance is very much a part of reflective practice, as we shall see in Part Three.

Exercise 1.1

What access to research evidence do you have? If this is limited, what can you (personally and collectively with your colleagues) do to seek to improve the situation?

Points to ponder

➤ How can you make sure that, when pressures are mounting, you are still able to avoid slipping into a mechanistic or reductionist approach?

➤ What steps are you able to take to ensure that you are managing risks as effectively as possible?
➤ Do you have strategies in place to promote empowerment rather than dependency?
➤ Do you know how to get access to summaries of relevant research findings?
➤ Do you have opportunities to discuss the above issues with colleagues?

Chapter 2
Law and Regulation

In order to understand contemporary care management practice, it is necessary to explore the legal context of community care, with a particular emphasis on regulation and quality assurance. The specific issues to be covered here are:

- an overview of the legal and political context of community care;
- a consideration of the restructuring of welfare;
- the impact of regulatory processes; and
- the role of quality assurance and different approaches to it.

The aim is not to provide a detailed account of the law and its implications, but rather to provide a critical analysis of the contemporary legal and regulatory context so that this can act as a foundation on which to build your own understanding of the complexities of these issues. In this respect, the aim is not to provide simple answers, but rather to offer 'food for thought' to encourage and support a critically reflective approach to these aspects of the context in which community care practices take place.

In relation to law and regulation there is a vast and complex technical knowledge base. However, it is not our intention to try and squeeze all of it into one relatively short account. Instead we shall pick out a number of key issues, as we see them, and use them as illustrative of the wider knowledge domain of this subject. We begin by briefly setting the current situation within its historical context.

The historical background

The role of the state in social welfare has traditionally been divided into three main roles:

- *the provision of services* – the provision of residential homes, day centres, home care and so on;
- *the funding of services* – the provision of grant funding for voluntary organisations, such as Age Concern, MIND and Women's Aid; and
- *the regulation of services* – registration, inspection and quality assurance in relation to state, voluntary and private services.

However, the development of New Right ideology in the last quarter of the twentieth century saw significant shifts in the balance of these three roles. The direct provision of services became a far less well-established part of state activity. The introduction of the purchaser/provider split and the emphasis on the brokerage of services in community care was certainly part of this shift. However, it was not the only one. Others included: the sale of council house properties; a lessening of the role of local education authorities and greater autonomy for individual schools; the use of private services, such as Group 4 in the provision of penal services; and a greater role for the private sector in health care provision.

This shift reflected the political ideology associated with the Conservative government in the UK under Thatcher and Major and the Republican government in the United States under Reagan. A key part of this ideology was a change of emphasis in the role of the state – moving away from what was perceived as 'the Nanny State' (which was criticised for encouraging dependency) towards an 'enabling' state (one which supported initiative, enterprise and endeavour). Of course, as with any ideology, this was a highly simplified version of reality and failed to take account of the complexities of the situation.

One significant result of this shift away from direct service provision was the placing of greater emphasis on the other two roles, funding and regulation. In terms of funding, one significant change was the development of service level agreements in place of grant funding. That is, instead of voluntary organisations requesting grant funding from social services departments (SSDs) in general terms, it became necessary for voluntary bodies to enter into specific contracts to provide identified services to an agreed specification and standard for the agreed time span of the contract. This change had (at least) two major effects: i) it gave SSDs (as an arm of the state) a greater say in the shaping of services provided by the voluntary sector; and ii) it provided a motivation for voluntary organisations to tailor their activities more closely to the SSDs' agendas (and a degree of tension for those organisations which preferred not to dovetail with local authority interests).

In terms of regulation, the pattern was similar – a much stronger emphasis on the state's role in regulating its own services and those provided by the voluntary and private sectors. This manifested itself in more efforts and resources being channelled into monitoring and inspection regimes and practices. The development of the Audit Commission was one example of this shift – a shift that can still be seen to be taking place in the early part of this century (as we shall note in more depth below).

Exercise 1.2

In what ways are you regulated in your current work? Can you identify what safeguards are in place to ensure that work undertaken meets specified requirements?

While the professed approach to welfare services of the Blair governments of 1997 and 2001 is generally presented as a move away from the New Right ideological underpinnings of the previous Conservative government, it none the less has much in common. That is, although the move away from direct funding towards greater control and regulation has its roots in one political ideology, the emergence of Blair's 'Third Way' has not made significant changes to the balance of the three roles of provision, funding and regulation of services. The 'Third Way' refers to a middle ground in between state socialism (the aspiration of the traditional left) on the one hand, and unfettered market capitalism on the other (the aspiration of the right).

Jordan (2000) makes an important point when he argues that social work is highly consistent with Blair's Third Way politics, even though social work is not mentioned in the social inclusion agenda that forms part of the Third Way:

> On the face of it, there should be an easy fit between the values underpinning New Labour's programme and those that drive social work practice. Tony Blair's own account of the Third Way (1998) and his political speeches (1996, 1999) emphasise equal value, autonomy, responsibility and community; his government aims to shift the culture of our society towards enabling individuals to contribute more and to give higher priority to the needs of others. The strong promotion of social inclusion as a policy goal seems to offer a particular opportunity for social work, since its low status under the previous regime was so closely connected with the exclusion of its clientele. Yet, the government's reforming and modernising agenda makes no mention of social work, except as a target for improving standards and new systems of quality control. (p. 141)

It seems that the emphasis on the state in general and social services departments in particular playing the roles of funders and regulators rather than providers is likely to continue for the foreseeable future. The emphasis on funding rather than providing is entirely consistent with the ethos of care management, while the emphasis on regulation is consistent with the current major concerns with inspection and quality assurance – themes to be explored in more detail below.

Practice Focus 1.3

Mark had been a care manager for a considerable number of years. He felt confident in his role and less experienced workers looked to him for advice and support. He was used to grappling with the dilemmas that this type of work faced him with and was trusted by his manager to perform competently and relatively independently. One morning he was called into the team leader's office and asked to justify a decision he had made some months earlier when he had arranged for a ninety-year-old man with dementia to be admitted to a residential home. Mark was told that an investigation was taking place following a complaint made to the inspectorate by the man's nephew. The team manager was satisfied with Mark's argument that he had made the decision following a thorough analysis of the risks involved and research into the man's competence to make decisions. He felt reassured that he had made a competent decision in the circumstances and felt relieved that he had his manager's support on this matter. However, the incident brought home to him that, however experienced he felt himself to be, his work remained open to scrutiny by regulatory bodies beyond his own immediate work environment.

Part of the process that has led to the shifting emphases has been an undermining of the professional basis of social work practice in general and of care management in particular. A significant theme that has therefore emerged from the changes described here is a greater tension between bureaucratic control and professional autonomy. This is therefore another theme that will be explored in this chapter.

The legal basis of community care

Of course, the central plank of community care legislation is the National Health Service and Community Care Act 1990 (NHSCCA). However, we need to remember that this is by no means the only aspect of the legal base worthy of attention when it comes to community care. For example, there are many other pieces of legislation that have a bearing on community care practice, some very long-established (the Mental Health Act 1983, for example) and others much more recent in origin (the Human Rights Act 1998, for example), while new developments seem to be occurring all the time (the development of national standards, for example).

Exercise 1.3

What pieces of legislation are you aware of which have a significant bearing on your work in community care? Compare notes with a colleague to see whether there are any you have missed.

The law provides a major part of the foundation on which practice is based but, of course, the law is not sufficient in itself, as it does not and cannot provide definitive solutions to the problems practitioners face on a daily basis. Linked to this is the importance of interpretation. That is, the relationship between the law and practice is not so clear cut as to rule out an important role for interpretation:

Although the influence of law and policy is very strong indeed, laws and policies have to be *interpreted* – they do not spell out in fine detail what needs to be done. For example, the NHS and Community Care Act 1990 speaks of 'people who are in need of community care services', but this is a very imprecise term that requires a great deal of interpretation. What exactly does 'in need of community care services' mean? How do we determine who is, and who is not, in need of such services? These are matters that have to be addressed directly in concrete situations, rather than dealt with at a generalized abstract level. Such matters are resolved at a very practical day-to-day level as social workers go about their business. (Thompson, 2000b, p. 45)

In terms of dealing with the legal basis of community care, it is therefore important to strike the right balance between, on the one hand, the major significance of the law and the disastrous results that can arise if we fail to take account of its requirements or to exercise its powers responsibly and, on the other, the need for interpretation and the exercise of professional discretion and autonomy.

Practice Focus 1.4

Sunita had been working with the Smith family for some months and had become very conscious of the tensions that existed between the family members. Their daughter, Gwenan, was 48-years old and had been left with profound physical and learning disabilities following an infection as a young baby. Gwenan's mother had provided all of the physical care that she required for all of her life and had consistently declined any help that had been offered. Sunita had become very concerned, about both Mrs Smith's health and indications that her declining ability to provide such an intensive level of care was leading to the development of pressure sores on Gwenan's body. She suspected that Gwenan's mother was under pressure from her husband not to accept any help, as he appeared to resent her involvement, and she often heard him instructing Mrs Smith to tell Sunita to go away and stop interfering. Sunita felt torn in several different directions by this case. On the one hand she knew that she had a duty in law to protect Gwenan's interests, but on the other hand she was also required by legislation to consider the right of her mother, as a carer, to support in her role. Back at the office she picked up a paper about the implications of the Human Rights Act 1998 and realised that Article 8 relating to privacy and family life might also have some relevance to the dilemma she faced and the confusion she was beginning to feel about what needed to inform her next move.

Developments in law and policy

Largely as a result of the shifts in political ideology discussed earlier, there have been very many developments in law and policy relating to community care in recent years and more developments 'in the pipeline'. We cannot realistically expect to cover all of these here. Our task, therefore, is to present brief details of a number of key developments so that we can sketch out an overall picture of the significant changes in law and policy that we are witnessing and will continue to witness for some time to come yet.

The Community Care (Direct Payments) Act 1996

When it came into effect in 1997, this Act gave local authorities the power to make financial payments directly to those people who had been assessed as being in need of community care services (except for permanent residential or nursing care), in place of those community care services. There was no compulsion, in that the Act gave local authorities the power to do so, but fell short of imposing a duty on them to offer this option. Where a local authority makes a payment directly to a person so that they can make arrangements that they, themselves, feel are appropriate to meet their needs, it becomes absolved of its responsibility to provide services, as long as they deem the arrangements made by the recipient (or a nominated carer or agent) to be effective and suitable. This places an onus on local authorities to ensure that regular monitoring and review take place. While the Act promotes independence and choice, it also allows local authorities to retain a degree of control in terms of their need to ensure that public funds are being used wisely and fairly.

It is an intention of this legislation that only those deemed able to manage their own arrangements be offered the direct payments facility as an option. It gives local authorities the right to refuse applicants who they deem unlikely to be able to manage the increased responsibilities that accompany the potential for greater independence, including the need to be accountable to the local authority for how the money allocated is being spent. Guidance warns against making assumptions about the ability of whole groups of people to cope with the rigours of managing direct payments, but the Act itself excluded anyone aged over 65 years from taking part. Following pressure from a number of sources, in 2000 the right to be considered as a recipient of direct payments was extended to older people, answering some of the concern about the discriminatory nature of the original legislation. Glasby and Littlechild (2002) remind us that care needs to be taken to ensure that the benefits of direct payment schemes are extended to all service user groups if equality of opportunity is to be maintained.

The Human Rights Act 1998

This Act was implemented on 2 October 2000. It makes the European Convention on Human Rights (ECHR) part of UK law. Therefore where there are breaches of human rights, which previously needed to be taken to the European Court of Human Rights (in Strasbourg), these can now be dealt with in the domestic courts across the UK. The Act applies to what are referred to as 'public authorities', a term broadly defined to include any organisation which fulfils a public duty and therefore clearly applies to those organisations involved in community care. The term also applies to courts and tribunals.

However, this is not simply a step to make the task of addressing human rights issues more convenient. It is also intended that a philosophy of human rights should become part of the culture of the UK legal systems and even of UK society more broadly. As Crompton and Thompson (2000) comment:

> The Government's broad aim in introducing the Act is to make a major contribution towards creating a society in which people's rights and responsibilities are balanced. As Straw (2000) puts it: 'A proper balance between the rights of the individual and the needs of the wider community lies at the heart of the ECHR'. The Act seeks to import that European commitment into domestic law. (p. 2.35)

This is an ambitious aim but one which has received a lot of government support. One very important way in which the Act seeks to influence the overall culture of law and society is through its effect on other pieces of legislation. The important point to note here is that the Human Rights Act 1998 does not only operate directly as an Act of Parliament, it also has an influence on other acts. This is because other pieces of legislation must be interpreted in ways that are compatible with the Human Rights Act. That is, where there is more than one way of interpreting a law, the interpretation chosen must be compatible with the requirements of the new act. In other words, where there is a possible conflict between an existing piece of legislation and the new Act, the human rights perspective must prevail. If necessary, in some cases Acts of Parliament will be changed to bring them into line with a culture of human rights.

Practice Focus 1.5

Clare worked in a hospital-based team and, for the most part, worked with adults with HIV or Aids. The team felt they needed to update themselves on relevant legislation and a training day was arranged so that they could consider the implications of the Human Rights Act 1998 for the work they undertook. The trainer highlighted Article 5 – 'the right to liberty and security of the person' – as an important aspect to consider in their work. Reflecting on her existing casework, Clare began to see that she needed to take this piece of legislation into account where people left weakened by physical illness became more vulnerable to physical, emotional and financial abuse. She could identify one particular situation in which a young woman, already the victim of physical violence from her partner, had been subjected to increasingly violent attacks as her condition worsened and the pressures on him increased. Aware of her terminal condition, Clare felt that the matter of protection should be taken out of the woman's hands, as she was clearly the victim of abuse and had no strength to 'fight her corner'. For this reason Article 5 seemed to offer the woman the right to protection – 'security of the person' – in law. While she was mulling this over, the trainer highlighted Article 8 – 'the right to respect for privacy and family life'. Clare realised that this could compromise the woman's right to protection from abuse. On the one hand the legislation promoted the right to be kept free from harm, but on the other it promoted the right not to have one's private and family life scrutinised. She had always been aware that different pieces of legislation often contradicted each other and that guidance was therefore not always helpful. What surprised her in this instance were the contradictions *within* this piece of legislation. While the training day was helpful, it served to highlight to the team that legislation based on rights is a complex arena, and one which they needed to engage with more fully if they were to work within the confines of the law.

Exercise 1.4

How does the Human Rights Act 1998 impact on your work? Are you able to identify particular Articles within the Act which have a direct bearing on your practice?

The Care Standards Act 2000

This piece of legislation aims to improve regulation in the provision of social care and private and voluntary health care. It is a wide-ranging Act, which covers many aspects of care provision and has a strong emphasis on matters relating to children's care and rights. It also has a number of implications for community care services and practice.

It established four regulatory councils for the social care workforce, based in England, Wales, Northern Ireland and Scotland.

The Act also introduces the idea of formal registration for social workers (parallel in some ways with the practice of nurse registration which has been in place for some time). In setting out the criteria for registration, for example, this legislation aims to ensure that those providing care for vulnerable people are competent to do so, and provides a basis for refusing entry to, or removing someone from, the register if they fail to meet the standards, which are based on the following criteria:

- appropriate physical and mental health;
- good character;
- qualification and training; and
- conduct and competence.

The Royal Commission on Long Term Care

Following a long and detailed investigation into the existing system of welfare provision for vulnerable older people, the Commission concluded that it is unnecessarily complex, inefficient and often leads to people being admitted to residential care. It proposed that, in future, this provision should be shared between the state and the individual and that clarity and equity should be guiding principles. To this end its two main recommendations were that:

- The costs of long-term care should be split between living costs, housing costs and personal care. Following assessment, the personal care element should be paid for from general taxation.
- The Government should establish a National Care Commission, with responsibility for monitoring demographic changes and levels of spending, ensuring that the system is accountable, takes the views of service users on board and is standardised by the use of national benchmarks.

At the time of writing, these recommendations have not been fully implemented.

Best value

The phrase 'best value' is one that has begun to have a major impact on social work in recent years. It is a concept that has developed, indirectly at least, from the New Right philosophy of 'rolling back the state', a lessening of reliance on state services, as discussed earlier. Part of this philosophy was the development of what came to be known as compulsory competitive tendering (CCT) – a system whereby certain services were put out to tender rather than provided directly by local government. This was a further example of the role of local government shifting from provider of services to funder and regulator of services.

One of the aims behind the CCT initiative was the introduction of supposed business-world efficiency (brought about by market forces) into the public sector. However, a major criticism of CCT which quickly emerged was that, while it may possibly have been effective in terms of cost containment, it was not effective in ensuring optimal outcomes. That is, what CCT produced for the most part was the cheapest level of service rather than the optimal level of service. To a large extent the notion of 'best value' is a reaction to this state of affairs. Its underlying principle is that local authorities should balance cost against quality to achieve the best outcomes possible within available resources. That is, it is not simply a matter of going for the cheapest options as these may save money in the short term but lead to much greater problems (and thus expense) in the medium to long term. Nor is it a matter of going for the highest quality of service that can be achieved as this may mean that services have to be rationed later in the financial year because resource considerations have not been given adequate attention. The best value approach is therefore geared towards achieving *the best possible service outcomes within available resources*. It can therefore be described as an attempt to ensure that professional quality concerns are balanced against financial management requirements.

Since April 2000 local authorities have been obliged to plan to provide their services in accordance with the principles of best value. Best value can be understood in terms of what have come to be known as the 'Four Cs of Best Value'. These are:

- **Challenging** why and how the service is best provided
- **Comparing** performance with others (including non-local government providers)
- **Competing** The authority must show that it has embraced the principles of fair competition in deciding who should deliver the service
- **Consulting** local service users and residents on their expectations about the service

The first C is an interesting one, in so far as it reflects one of the key issues to be discussed in Part Two – namely, the importance of systematic practice: keeping a clear focus and thus being explicit about what we are doing and why.

Joint reviews

The Joint Reviews initiative combines the approaches of those reporting on the effectiveness of services (for example, Social Services Inspectorate) and those concerned with ensuring that public money is spent wisely (the Audit Commission) to monitor the performance of individual local authorities.

The overall aim of Joint Reviews is to improve social services by highlighting where policies and practice are producing the most effective results and using this process to help authorities improve management practices and provide better services within a framework of securing value for money. Eight key principles guide the review process:

- *User focus*: seeking and taking note of the experience of recipients of services;
- *Partnership*: at all levels and across all agencies;
- *Inclusion*: involving all stakeholders and the sharing of lessons learned;
- *Based on evidence*: findings to be rooted in evidence;
- *Consistency*: applying principles of best practice to the team itself to ensure a common approach;
- *Corporacy*: looking at the performance of other local authority functions that contribute to social services, as well as social services departments themselves;
- *Development*: emphasising future potential and identifying an agenda for improvement; and
- *Openness*: publishing reports, both on individual authorities and annually on combined findings.

The NHS plan

The NHS Plan was published in 2000 within the context of the Government's intention to make the Health Service primary care-driven, rather than hospital-driven. The plan outlined the following intentions:

- An expansion in training – to significantly increase the number of doctors, nurses and other allied professions.
- The promotion of policy initiatives of relevance to older people, particularly in respect of managing the transition between hospital and home more effectively and efficiently.
- Closer integration of health and social care services through the expansion of primary care trusts, with an emphasis on moves to establish single legal bodies that would have responsibility for commissioning and managing all health and social care provision within a locality.

The NHS Plan also outlined an intention to establish a single assessment process for older people, to facilitate the assessment of health and social care without unnecessary duplication.

This list of developments should be more than enough to confirm that the community care law and policy arena is a dynamic one, changing in a number of ways in response to these various legal and policy initiatives. It is perhaps not surprising that a common complaint to be heard these days is of the stress associated with feeling lost in a whirlwind of major changes (Thompson et al., 1997). However, while change on such a massive scale brings significant pressures and challenges, it also brings major opportunities – openings for developing new approaches which avoid some of the problems of the past and build on the strengths that we have. We should recognise the size of the task we face in working our way through such an unstable landscape, but not allow ourselves to become defeatist and cynical by seeking to capitalise on the opportunities presented.

Although there clearly are opportunities arising, there are also dangers. One such danger is that of allowing the sea of changes to 'flood' us, to the point where we lose our focus and fall foul of drift. Times of major change are notorious for being times when the additional pressures lead people to forget their primary roles and the purposes they are seeking to fulfil. This brings us once again to systematic practice and the need to keep a clear focus on what we are trying to achieve, how we are trying to achieve it and how we will know when we have achieved it (see Part Two). We have to make sure that the turbulent times do not lead to the loss of a systematic approach to practice.

Practice Focus 1.6

Gary had been carrying an unusually high workload for several months. Two of his colleagues in the care management team had left their posts unexpectedly, and another was on long-term sick leave. He felt the relative isolation particularly keenly as he had welcomed the opportunity to share anxieties with them and help keep each other up to date with changes in policy or new guidelines. Over the last few weeks he had been working very long hours in an attempt to deal with a number of situations that had presented themselves as emergencies, and felt that his ongoing casework was being neglected. He was not happy with this situation, but felt that he had to 'keep the service afloat' by honouring the local authority's commitments in law. However, one particular incident brought home to him that his usually competent work was being compromised by this pressure. In the midst of dealing with a flood of referrals Gary took a frantic phone call from the manager of a hostel to say that she was evicting Eve, who had mental health and drug-related problems. In an attempt to deal with this matter quickly, Gary acted without investigating the issue or listening to Eve's perspective, and arranged a place at a different facility, which he later realised had been a totally inappropriate move, given the fragile state of Eve's mental health at that moment. When he finally took time to review his caseload he realised that he had allowed himself to be drawn into using expediency to solve problems rather than his usual planned and partnership-based approach. The disastrous effect on Eve's confidence proved to be a salutary lesson and he vowed that, however busy he became, he would always take time to ensure that he never again lost track of what he was trying to achieve with each individual service user.

The issues raised here, while by no means providing a comprehensive analysis of law and regulation, should none the less be sufficient to demonstrate clearly that community care has its roots in law as well as in social policy and welfare provision more broadly. It is important that this point is appreciated, as an adequate understanding of community care cannot be achieved without taking account of issues of law and regulation.

Points to ponder

➤ How clear are you about the legal and policy aspects of your work?
➤ How comfortable do you feel with them? What can you do to feel more comfortable?
➤ How will you manage to keep up to date with so many new developments?
➤ Do you have access to libraries, the Internet and so on?
➤ Are you clear about the implications of regulation and professional accountability for your practice?

Chapter 3
Working in Partnership

In this chapter we explore important issues relating to collaborating with other professionals as part of a multidisciplinary network, as well as working in tandem with service users and carers.

The term 'partnership' is one that has become very well established in recent years. Indeed, many would argue that it has achieved the status of a buzzword – that is, it has become a fashionable concept often used by people who have relatively little grasp of its meaning or its implications for practice. An important aim of this chapter is therefore to challenge its status as a buzzword and to replace this with a sound understanding of what the concept refers to and why it is so important in contemporary community care practice.

Although it is clearly one of the 'words of the moment', the term partnership does in fact have a long history. For example, the idea that professionals from different backgrounds should work together has been established for decades. A significant development in this regard was the Children Act 1989 which heralded an emphasis on the need for child care workers to work in partnership with children, their parents and other agencies involved in child care work (Thompson, 2002a). More recently, a new wave of emphasis on partnership has developed, closely linked to New Labour's emphasis on what they refer to as the Third Way (as discussed earlier). Powell et al. (2001) argue that partnership is part and parcel of the New Labour approach to public service. This means that partnership is an important means of trying to avoid an over-reliance on both the state as the foundation of public service and the market as a regulator and provider of social welfare. Partnership as a political and policy concept is an attempt to steer away from the traditional polarity of state and market.

This has had major implications for how community care services (and indeed public services as a whole) are organised and delivered. As Sullivan and Skelcher (2002) point out:

> A radical transformation is taking place in the way communities are governed. Funding and authority for the development and delivery of public policy are increasingly located in collaborative ventures, involving a range of governmental, business, voluntary and community agencies. These are most typically termed 'partnerships' and are found in all fields of public policy. Although an international phenomenon, the UK has undergone a major expansion of partnerships, many stimulated by central government and operating at the sub-national level. This change poses major challenges for the ways in which power and governmental activity are

understood, and for the practice of public service managers and others involved in collaborations. (p. xi)

They go on to argue that partnership is the 'new language of public governance' (p. 1). It is clearly, then, an important development in social policy which is having an impact on the direct level of practice.

Exercise 1.5

Can you identify any ways in which the 'third way' and its emphasis on partnerships between different organisations and sectors have had an impact on your work? What difference has it made? What benefits and what problems do you associate with this policy development?

The idea of partnership is therefore very much a major part of this new approach to public service delivery and, of course, community care is no exception to this. A major emphasis here is that of 'seamless service' involving close collaboration between health and social services personnel in matters relating to the community care needs of vulnerable adults. The need for people from different agencies to work closely together is now therefore firmly on the agenda at both policy and practice levels.

The development of the user participation movement has also played a significant part in emphasising the need for partnership, but this time, not only a partnership between professional agencies, but also one between service providers and service users and their carers. This helps us understand that there are three levels of partnership that we need to address: between service users and service providers, between service providers and carers, and the diverse range of collaborative arrangements between the various service providers within a multidisciplinary context. This module will address all three of these levels but, before doing so, will address the important and far from simple question of: What is partnership?

What is partnership?

At its simplest level, of course, partnership means working *with* people (rather than doing things *for* or *to* them). However, while this may be a good beginning to develop our understanding of what partnership is, it is far from adequate on its own.

Thompson (2000b) argues that partnership has now become established as one of social work's values. He describes it as an 'emancipatory value'. By this he means that it forms part of the development in recent years of forms of practice which seek to address discrimination and oppression. He contrasts partnership as a value with the more traditional approach in social work based on a medical model in which social care staff are expected to 'diagnose' the problem and develop a programme of treatment for resolving the difficulties identified. He argues that such a medical approach needs to be replaced by a partnership-based approach in which:

- Assessment of the situation is carried out in close co-operation with the client(s) and, where appropriate, the carer(s) – with a view to establishing agreement on the nature of the problem, the identified needs, the objectives to aim for and possible plans of action for responding to them.
- Intervention involves the relevant parties working together to take the necessary steps to resolve or minimise problems, to meet needs and to do whatever is needed to meet the agreed objectives.
- The situation is jointly reviewed at appropriate points and, ideally, jointly evaluated when the piece of work comes to an end. (p. 119)

This refers to working directly with service users and carers, but Thompson goes on to argue that the same model can be used at a broader level – for example, by involving service users and carers in the planning and evaluation of services, and even in such matters as the delivery of training.

Practice Focus 1.7

Liz was very concerned when she first met Mrs Williams. This was because Mrs Williams did not want to play an active part in the process. She simply kept saying: 'You know best, I'll go along with whatever you say'. However, Liz was only too aware of the importance of partnership and therefore set about trying to change the situation. She did not put Mrs Williams under undue pressure, but she did persist in trying to involve her in the process. Before long, she managed to use her skills to engage Mrs Williams and enable her to express her wishes and feelings. It was hard work getting to that point, but Liz was so glad that she did, partly because she gained a great deal of job satisfaction from it, and partly because she knew that this was a much sounder foundation on which to base her work with Mrs Williams, as this situation would be far less likely to break down than one that she had not been involved in planning and shaping.

In seeking to promote partnership, it is of course necessary to be clear about its benefits. These include:

- *Giving people voice*. Partnership allows people who might otherwise go unheard to have their say.
- *Mutual support*. Although partnership can bring tension and strife, it can also be an excellent source of mutual support for all involved.
- *It is more holistic*. There is less danger of the approach taken being one-sided or neglecting crucial aspects of the situation.

- *A forum for learning from each other*. Understanding different perspectives can be a tremendous source of learning and opportunities for broadening our horizons.
- *It involves sharing responsibility*. This can discourage the development of a blame culture and can encourage shared ownership of both problems and solutions.

Clearly, then, there are significant benefits to be gained by overcoming the difficulties and tensions involved in developing partnership-based approaches. Baxter and Toon (2001) capture well the positive nature of at least one aspect of partnership when, in discussing NHS reforms, they comment that:

> The move towards interprofessionalism is based upon the view that all participants bring equally knowledge and expertise from their professional and personal experience and that a 'diverse group can arrive at a place no individual and no like-minded group would have reached' (Davis, 2000). (p. 271)

Exercise 1.6

If you were to encounter difficulties in working in the way described above (for example, in working with someone with dementia or severe learning disabilities), what steps could you take to get round such obstacles?

Partnership, then, can be seen to operate at three separate but interconnected levels:

1. With clients: in identifying what needs to be done and taking the steps necessary to make it happen.
2. With carers: in identifying what role they can play in supporting the client and what support they may need for themselves.
3. With professional colleagues: within one's own agency and in other settings.

We shall return to these issues in Part Two when we explore what needs to be done to make partnership a reality at each of these three levels.

Points to ponder

➤ Is partnership a concept that you already feel comfortable with or is it something you are going to have to work on? If the latter, how do you plan to do so?
➤ What do you regard as your strengths when it comes to working in partnership with service users? And what do you see as your weaknesses or areas for development?

➤ What do you regard as the basic building blocks of successful partnership work with carers?

➤ How well developed are your negotiation skills? Are you able to negotiate effectively? That is, can you avoid both the tendency to attempt to coerce the other party(ies) into your way of thinking and the equally problematic tendency to 'duck the issue' of any conflict that needs to be resolved?

➤ How do you respond in situations characterised by conflict? If you are not confident about your ability to handle conflict constructively, what steps can you take to improve the situation?

Conclusion

Part One has sought to present an overview of the professional knowledge base underpinning community care, the theory that informs practice. In order to achieve this aim we have addressed three sets of issues: the nature and importance of care management as a central pillar of community care; the fundamental role of law and regulation; and the benefits of attempting to work in partnership.

This overview of key aspects of the theory base sets the scene for our discussions in Part Two of the vast array of practice issues associated with community care. We recommend that you now move on and read Part Two and then come back to Part One and re-read it in order to make sure that you are well equipped to link the elements of theory and practice together, for, as we shall see in Part Three when we discuss reflective practice, integrating theory and practice is a key part of developing and maintaining high standards of community care practice.

Part Two: Community Care Practice

Introduction

Part One summarised some key issues relating to the underpinning knowledge base as it applies to community care in general and care management in particular. Our task here is to draw out some of the implications of that knowledge base for day-to-day practice. We shall concentrate on five in particular, devoting a chapter to each:

Chapter 4: Risk management. Assessment and the subsequent co-ordination of care packages necessarily involve a range of risks. It is therefore important to have an understanding of at least the basics of risk assessment and risk management. These are complex issues and best not simply left to chance – indeed, that is the basis of risk management: leaving as little as possible to the vagaries of chance by anticipating hazardous situations and preparing for them.

Chapter 5: Systematic practice. Drift and a lack of focus are recognised problems that often arise when people are in highly pressurised situations. Systematic practice (that is, being clear at all times what we are doing and why we are doing it) is therefore an important antidote to these problems. Adopting a focused, systematic approach will not only make us more efficient and effective, it will also have a positive effect on both confidence and morale.

Chapter 6: Empowerment. There is little point providing services for people when they can be helped to solve their own problems and meet their own needs without recourse to such services. Helping people gain greater control over their lives is therefore an important feature of high-quality care management. Consequently, we need to avoid the common assumption that empowerment is not possible in pressurised circumstances of resource shortfall. We would argue that the opposite is the case: the more pressurised the circumstances, the more important empowerment becomes.

Chapter 7: Regulation and professional accountability. Community care workers need to operate in the context of law and policy in which their work is regulated and subject to professional accountability. This chapter explores the implications of this for practice.

Chapter 8: Making partnership work. The importance of working in partnership has already been stressed. Here we explore how this can be made a reality as far as possible. This involves looking at how we can form good working relationships with clients, carers and colleagues.

However, before beginning our discussions of these issues it is important to re-emphasise a point made in Part One, namely the fact that care management is more than an administrative process.

While care management is in some ways different from traditional social work, it is a mistake to assume that it is not a form of social work. As we saw in Part One, social work knowledge, skills and values have an important part to play if we are to avoid care management becoming a mechanical process of rationing scarce resources. Care management is a skilled and challenging role, and so we need to be as well prepared as we can.

Exercise 2.1

What knowledge, skills and values do you feel you are drawing upon in undertaking care management work? How do these help you achieve high standards of practice?

The point was made in Part One that some people have interpreted the community care reforms in very narrow terms and thus see care management as little more than an administrative exercise involving the routine gathering of basic information, form filling and the rationing of scarce resources. It is our view that this narrow interpretation is dangerous as it means that the needs of vulnerable people come second to administrative process – thereby contributing to processes that could have discriminatory and thus oppressive outcomes (see Part Three).

Practice Focus 2.1

Following a review of the paperwork used by Karen's team in the Adult Services Department, a new assessment form was introduced. It contained a checklist and some of her colleagues commented on how useful it was when undertaking assessments of need in people's homes. However, Karen was not so enthusiastic, as she felt it focused too strongly on physical limitations at the expense of other, less tangible needs. She was reminded of a visit she made to a 60-year-old man who had been referred to the team by neighbours because of self-neglect. Although he had insisted that his only need was for someone to bring him a meal and wash his clothes, Karen felt that his needs went beyond the physical. After a number of visits, the man opened up to her that he had been devastated by the loss of his friend, who had died of cancer a few months earlier. They rarely met in person, but his letters had made him feel a sense of connection with the world when he was experiencing the periods of depression to which he was prone. Karen wondered whether this new checklist would have prompted her colleagues to think about need in that sort of context.

It is therefore important to recognise the potential for care management to conceptualise social workers more as administrators of a system geared towards managing scarce resources than as professional problem solvers, advocates for vulnerable adults and champions of social justice. So, how can we ensure that these important aspects of our role as social workers are incorporated into the changing ethos and working patterns, rather than lost to other priorities and obligations? Keeping a clear focus on the *purpose* of our intervention is one strategy – that is to say, keeping a focus on what we are trying to achieve in social work terms, as managers of packages of care. Systematic practice is an approach that can be very helpful in this regard. We shall return to this subject in Chapter 5.

Chapter 4
Risk Management

Aspects of the theory of risk were discussed in Part One. Here our focus shifts to how we relate the insights of such theory to practice.

While risk management is something that community care workers deal with all the time in a work context, it is not *just* a workplace concept. Risk is something we deal with on a daily basis in our home lives too. We cannot get through a day without weighing up the risks and benefits involved in any course of action we propose. For example, we might want to stay in bed all day when it is cold outside, but realise that we risk losing our jobs or our health if we do that, and make our decisions on the basis of the likely consequences of any decisions we make. We are not always aware of these deliberations, but they take place none the less, and not just about issues that are overtly dangerous, like whether to go sky-diving or not. Virtually every step we take and every activity we pursue involves some degree of risk, and these risks need weighing up in the face of alternative strategies. If we were conscious of these processes we would probably never move or speak for fear of possible negative outcomes, and so most of us manage to find a workable balance where risk taking is concerned. That is, we accept that we have to take risks sometimes in order to live our lives in the manner that we choose to live them.

In other words we are all living 'at risk' in one way or another, even though we do not always take the advice we are given – for example, on smoking, dietary choices and driving at speed. We tend to develop some degree of competence in assessing risks that may go beyond acceptable boundaries, but some people are especially vulnerable to particular risks (for example, someone with a heart condition). Risk management can be difficult at times, but it remains part of everyday lifestyle choices.

There are, however, certain circumstances where risk taking can legitimately be denied or curtailed by others – for example, health and safety requirements in relation to the use of dangerous machinery or legal requirements in relation to driving while under the influence of alcohol.

While there are, then, certain circumstances in which risk taking can legitimately be denied, this is not to say that anyone can deny anyone else the opportunity to take risks. A person's right to take risks is not absolute, but there has to be a good reason for another person to interfere in that right. This means that, in a community care context, we have to be careful not to interfere in a person's risk-taking behaviour without proper justification. What, then, constitutes 'proper justification'? The following are the main areas:

- *Where the individual concerned is placing one or more other people at serious risk of harm.*

This may involve a criminal matter where one person's behaviour is endangering another – for example, where threatening behaviour is involved. However, such situations have to be weighed up very carefully.

- *Where, owing to a mental health problem, the individual concerned is placing him- or herself or other people at serious risk of harm.*

This may be a matter for an approved social worker under the Mental Health Act 1989 to assess what action needs to be taken. Again the situation has to be weighed up very carefully.

However, it is important to note that neither of the above sets of circumstances involves a situation where the individual concerned chooses (in the absence of mental incapacity or disorder) to place him- or herself at risk of serious harm. Individuals have the right to live 'at risk' if they so choose in situations where their capacity to make informed choices has not been diminished in some way. This is a very significant issue as relatives and other concerned people can put workers under considerable pressure to reduce the level of risk a person chooses to live at. It is important to recognise that risks are sometimes overstated in welfare settings (Manthorpe and Stanley, 2002), and so we have to be careful not to bow to inappropriate pressure to overrule someone's right to take risks.

How, then, can we seek to ensure that risk issues are managed appropriately? This is a big question that could justify a whole book in its own right. However, for present purposes we would propose:

- *Balance risks against rights*. Be very careful not to allow concerns about risk to infringe an individual's rights.
- *Balance positives against negatives*. There is much to be gained from risk taking, in so far as key aspects of an individual's identity are often linked to taking risks (sports, work activities and so on). Having a narrow focus on just reducing risks can be counterproductive – that is, it can do more harm than good.
- *Assess risk carefully*. Risk assessment is a complex business, and there are various models that can be used (see Part Four for guidance on further reading that can help you develop the knowledge and skills required for effective risk assessment).

An important point to emphasise is that, by its very nature, risk assessment is something that we will get wrong from time to time. Dealing with risk issues is not an exact science. We can do everything we reasonably can to ensure a balanced and helpful approach to risk, but still have to face up to the fact that things can go terribly wrong at times. It is at such times that being able to demonstrate that risk assessment has taken place will stand us in good stead.

Exercise 2.2

What risk factors do you commonly encounter in your work? How do you recognise these? How do you assess their significance in particular cases?

Chapter 5
Systematic Practice

The systematic practice framework (Thompson, 2000a, 2002a) is one which advocates that we keep a clear focus to the work we are undertaking, which then helps us to see that, as care managers, we use our professional skills to make professional judgements about how best to manage risk and need, rather than just rationing and handing out scarce resources in a routinised and bureaucratic manner. So, what is systematic practice?

This is an approach which seeks to challenge practice that is vague and unfocused, and which has a tendency to 'drift' without any real plan or direction. Apart from the potential for such practice to fall wide of the mark in terms of meeting needs of service users, this lack of focus can lead to problems when social workers are called on to justify their actions or decisions. All too often this vagueness is commented on negatively by investigators of complaints and inquiries that follow from court cases where social work competence is challenged. One of the present authors has encountered this problem on a number of occasions in his own work as an independent consultant

The benefits of developing systematic practice can be seen to have a number of important benefits. In particular, it can help us avoid a number of significant pitfalls, not least the following:

- Care management involves juggling lots of different balls in the air – time is precious, so getting sidetracked is costly. It is all too well known how a seemingly straightforward referral can turn out to involve a complex set of issues requiring a lot of time and expertise. The danger here is that, without a clear understanding of what your role is, what the problem is, and how you can intervene most effectively in that particular situation, it is very easy to get drawn into issues that are not really social work concerns. This is not necessarily a deliberate ploy on the part of other professionals or anxious service users but once identified as a key person, care managers often find themselves presented with any or all of the problems that manifest themselves, regardless of whether they are best suited, or required by law, to respond to them. Having a clear systematic approach can help to avoid this.

- Clarity about what we are doing can help in terms of workload management. Being responsible for the management of packages of care means having to respond to emergencies, which can impact quite seriously on other planned work and obligations. Priorities are constantly being negotiated and renegotiated and thought patterns interrupted in the process. Without a clear and explicit sense of direction and purpose it becomes difficult to refocus on a particular piece of work once you have judged it appropriate to make it your next priority. Without a clear sense of role and direction there is a danger that work that should be taking priority is overlooked, key deadlines missed and the significance of changes in circumstance lost. Vagueness and drift can lead to the workload being perceived as unmanageable – with the potential for stress that ensues from feeling out of control (Thompson, 1999).

- Evaluation is a keystone of good practice, but one which is often overlooked in the pressure to 'get things done' (Shaw, 1996). In care management there is a strong focus on securing and monitoring services – on getting responses to assessed need organised quickly. Under pressure to get things done it can be all too easy to overlook the need to take a few steps back to consider how well the work has been done – to evaluate what has and has not worked, whether all parties have been satisfied with the outcome and so on. This process becomes difficult, if not impossible, if we are not able to identify clearly what it is that we have set out to do in the first place. How can we tell whether we have achieved our aims if we have not established what they were in the first place?

- Confidence is, of course, an important part of effective practice, and this can be seen to apply in two senses. First, there is self-confidence – the self-belief we need to help us rise to the challenges involved. Second, there is the confidence that service users and carers need to have in us if we are to form the trusting relationships on which effective practice is built. If we are unfocused in our work and allow drift to creep in to what we are doing, we are unlikely to feel confident about our own abilities to achieve high standards of practice and it is extremely unlikely that others will have confidence in us.

These are only some of the pitfalls that a vague and unsystematic approach can lead us into. You may be able to think of others or at least be able to appreciate how dangerous it can be to practise without any real idea of what you are aiming for in your interventions and why. So, how can a systematic framework help? It does so by setting you the task of asking three questions of your practice at the outset of any form of intervention – and this includes care management:

1. What are you trying to achieve?
2. How are you going to achieve it?
3. How will you know when you have achieved it?

Let us explore each of these in turn.

What are you trying to achieve?

This is the goal-setting stage, at which objectives are identified. It is all too easy to rush in with solutions without really understanding what the problem is. Without asking this question and giving ourselves time to think through the complexities (for example, do I and the service user have the same perspective on what constitutes the problem?), we may not be able to formulate a clear picture of what outcomes we are hoping for. Identifying what it is you are trying to achieve sounds like a solitary activity and, indeed, time spent in clarifying the issues for yourself is likely to be time well spent, but it is important to remember that goal setting needs to be seen in the context of partnership, a point to which we shall return below. Responding to this first question involves working together to set the agenda and to identify a set of objectives that are attainable.

In relation specifically to care management what this approach has to offer is a focus on identifiable outcomes. That is, it helps us to avoid care management simply becoming the rationing of scarce resources.

How are you going to achieve it?

Once the targets for our intervention have been identified, we need to think about how we can reach those targets. That is, we need to plan a route which will lead us to what we have identified as the goals to be reached. Where the previous activity in relation to the first question was described as goal setting, this phase is one of strategy setting. The wisdom of making objectives shared and attainable becomes evident here, in that commitment to working towards objectives is unlikely to be maintained if the road is too rocky, or the journey too long and without tangible results. As a social worker the range of interventions and theoretical perspectives you can draw upon in order to achieve your objectives is extensive – part of being a social worker is judging which approach will be useful in a particular set of circumstances.

This framework does not offer specific solutions – there is obviously no one strategy that will provide the answer for every problem. Indeed, it recognises that even when strategies have been agreed, they often need to be changed in the light of new circumstances – plans of action are not set in stone. What it does do is remind us of the necessity of having a strategy in the first place and of making it explicit. Taking time out on a regular basis to revisit the problem and to ask the question 'how am I going to achieve the goals we have set?' will help to revise or reaffirm the chosen strategies and therefore keep a focus on what is potentially a messy and unpredictable field of work.

It is an approach which also comes into its own when we become 'stuck' and cannot seem to see the wood for the trees. Sometimes we can concentrate so much on getting things *done* and getting them done to deadlines, or in response to emergencies that might leave vulnerable people without the support they need, that we lose sight of the *how* and *why* of what we are doing. It is understandable that our thinking can become 'muddied' in times of increased pressure, but using a systematic approach can help keep a check by returning us to the problem and strategy setting, thereby guarding against the 'headless chicken' approach which can result otherwise.

Practice Focus 2.2

Sanjay was asked by his manager during supervision to clarify why he was continuing to keep Mrs Cargill's case open. Although he had not reviewed the case for a number of weeks because of other priorities, Sanjay was quickly able to identify the issues and respond that the case was still open because the objectives he had identified with Mrs Cargill and her husband some time earlier had not yet been attained. When thinking about how to respond to the initial referral, Sanjay had decided to approach the matter systematically – setting the problem, deciding on a strategy for achieving the desired outcome and defining what a successful outcome would look like. In this case, he knew he would have achieved his aims when Mrs Cargill was happy to let support workers supervise her while her husband took time out from his caring responsibilities to visit his friends. As he had not yet achieved what he had set out to, he was able to justify keeping the case open to his manager. Being able to account for his actions and judgements in this way gave Sanjay the feeling that, while he was very busy, he was also in control.

The implementation of the NHS and Community Care Act 1990 has to be recognised as not simply a shift to managing or brokering service provision. It also involved an emphasis on the need to be creative, to look beyond existing services. A systematic approach can help us in this regard by encouraging us to think laterally about how needs can be met, how problems can be solved and how progress can be made, rather than settle for relying on standard responses or routine reactions.

How will you know when you have achieved it?

This sounds like a question you should ask yourself at the end of an intervention, but that is not the case. The question needs to be asked at the same time as the first two, as its purpose is to test out whether the first two questions have been adequately explored. For example, are the objectives you have identified measurable? Are you able to conceptualise at the outset what success will look like at the end? If the answer is no, then you have no way of identifying whether you have succeeded in your aims or not. The following example might help to clarify the point here.

Jack, an adult with learning disabilities, has been living with his sister for many years and they have been mutually supportive. She dies suddenly and you are asked to intervene. You answer the first two questions as follows:

- *What are you trying to achieve?* The objective is to help Jack cope through this difficult time.
- *How are you going to achieve it?* The strategy is to visit regularly and check on whether he is coping on his own.
- *How will you know whether you have achieved it?* This is where it becomes evident that the objectives have been rather too vague. Are you able to say what success would look like here? How would you know whether you had helped him through? How would you know when or whether to withdraw? Being unable to answer this third question should then alert you to the need to refocus on objectives and strategies.

A more effective approach in terms of this scenario might look as follows:

- *What are you trying to achieve?* The goal is to boost his confidence and improve his daily living skills to the extent that he is able to live on his own in relative safety. The objectives are to ensure that he can budget for and prepare his meals, manage the laundry and manage his finances without becoming unduly anxious.
- *How are you going to achieve it?* To arrange for Jack to have a support worker who will be present at mealtimes, accompany him to the laundrette and supermarket once a week and help him to collect his pension and pay his bills. The level of support in these tasks will become less intensive as Jack's skill and competence increase.
- *How will you know when you have achieved it?* This third question now becomes answerable. I will know I have achieved my objectives when Jack is carrying out these tasks independently without endangering himself or anyone else.

Exercise 2.3

Think about a client you are currently working with (or have worked with recently). Ask yourself the three key questions of systematic practice in relation to this situation. If you find it easy to answer them repeat the exercise with another service user and so on, to enable you to become accustomed to this method of practice. If you do not find it easy to answer the three questions, consider what you will need to do in future to make sure you are able to adopt such a systematic approach.

Practice Focus 2.3

Karl had been working with Martin, a young man with muscular dystrophy, to manage his care package. Martin lived in his own flat, with the aid of several support workers who provided round the clock care between them. Martin wanted to be as independent as possible, and his carers respected this, only doing what he requested of them. On several occasions Martin had asked for their help in visiting employment agencies and various government departments in order to talk about benefit entitlements and job prospects, but the experiences had left him physically and emotionally exhausted. After these attempts at securing himself a future and a place in the world, Martin felt demoralised and the carers reported to Karl that he was becoming withdrawn and losing his independent spirit. On his next visit, Karl showed Martin how he could visit the websites of these agencies, access the information he needed in order to make decisions about his life, and converse with others via electronic technology. Before long, Martin was taking control of his life, to the point where he was arranging to interview a new carer without the others even being aware of it. Karl saw this as an excellent outcome, in that he had been able to empower Martin without any consequence to his responsibilities as his care manager.

Chapter 6

Empowerment

The term 'empowerment' is one that we encountered in Part One, where the point was made that it can often be used in an uncritical way. Empowerment involves helping people gain greater control over their lives. This can be seen to operate at three levels, personal, cultural and structural:

- *Personal*. Individuals can be helped to gain greater control over their lives in a variety of ways – for example, through the enhancement of confidence and self esteem.
- *Cultural*. Discriminatory assumptions and stereotypes can be challenged in an attempt to break down an oppressive culture in which the values and interests of dominant groups are presented as normal and natural. Empowerment at this level is therefore concerned with 'consciousness-raising', becoming aware of ideologies premised on inequality.
- *Structural*. Power relations are rooted in the structure of society and so empowerment at this level must involve the eradication, in the long term, of structured inequalities. This involves a collective political response, a concerted programme of action for social change. (Thompson, 2003a, p. 77)

Let us look a little more closely at each of these in terms of what they mean in a community care context:

- *Personal*. An important issue here is making sure that we do not encourage dependency. A significant danger is that well-meaning professionals and other carers can, often unwittingly, *dis*empower people by focusing too much on providing services and not enough on helping people to meet their own needs or solve their own problems.
- *Cultural*. We need to make sure that we do not allow stereotypes and other assumptions at the cultural level to stand in the way of partnership. For example, we need to make sure that we do not assume that older people are not capable of making their own decisions or that disabled people cannot speak for themselves.
- *Structural*. The workings of power are both very subtle and very influential. It is important that we do not act in ways that reinforce structural power relations – for example, by failing to take account of the problems associated with racial disadvantage or sexual discrimination.

In addition we need to recognise that empowerment *is* a matter of challenging the perception that the power rests solely with the professional worker. In a care management context, as in any other, all parties have some degree of power (even if it is only the power of refusal or the power to make a complaint). We need to adopt a sophisticated approach to analysing power dynamics so that we can (i) use available power resources for the positive benefit of clients; and (ii) counter the inappropriate (and thus potentially oppressive) use of power where necessary.

If we are not careful, what can very easily happen is that clients *defer* to the professionals involved and thus do not use what power they have. It is important, then, that we do not allow this to lead to a situation in which we are colluding with someone's self-disempowerment. We need to be sensitive to the tendency for certain groups of people to internalise oppression – that is, to take on board negative assumptions about themselves (for example, the internalised ageist assumption that older people are not important can manifest itself as a reluctance to accept offers of help). Colluding with internalised oppression is not, of course, a form of empowerment.

What *is* a form of empowerment is the willingness to work in partnership – to move away from the traditional 'we know best' mentality to an approach premised on agreeing what problems need to be solved and how they can best be solved. This is a topic to which we shall return below.

Exercise 2.4

What does the word 'empowerment' mean to you? What does it conjure up in your mind? How important a role does it play in your day-to-day practice? Are there any steps you can take to make sure that it does not get lost in the pressure of work?

Chapter 7
Regulation and Professional Accountability

Social work is regarded as a 'semi-profession', in so far as it is more closely constrained by agency requirements than the 'full' or traditional professions of law, medicine, architecture and so on. However, all professional groups, whether traditional or semi-professions, need to be regulated to a certain extent. This involves ensuring as far as possible that:

- standards of practice are at least meeting a basic minimum and preferably as high a level as possible;
- ethical requirements are being met; and
- continuous learning and development take place.

Partly as a result of government agendas and partly in response to crises within social work (the events leading to the publication of the Waterhouse Report relating to abuse in children's homes, for example), recent years have seen a new, stronger approach to regulation. Davies (2000) captures the situation well when she points out that:

> Those working in health and social care have found their work being increasingly scrutinised from outside the workplace as well as in it. External audits and inspections have proliferated. New techniques have been devised for measuring output, assessing effectiveness and questioning whether established procedures and patterns of work represent value for money. Governments . . . have become more and more determined to set national standards and national frameworks for public service delivery. (p. 297)

This has manifested itself in a number of ways, such as the development of care standards bodies (inspectorates and care councils) which have a direct bearing on monitoring standards. The following bodies also have a role to play in regulating community care.

- *Commissioner for Local Administration (Local Government Ombudsman).* The commissioner can investigate complaints of maladministration against local authorities. There is an equivalent commissioner for the Health Service.
- *Equality commissions.* In addition to the above, there are bodies such as the Commission for Racial Equality, the Equal Opportunities Commission and the Disability Rights Commission which can become involved where breaches of anti-discrimination law may be an issue.

This is not a complete list, but it should be enough to establish that community care practice is subject to various forms of regulation. Some people oversimplify the situation and argue that, because of this extensive regulation, community care practice is no longer a professional activity. However, this fails to recognise the necessity for professional practice. As Jordan (1990) comments:

> it is because situations are complex and susceptible to a number of interpretations that the judgement, discretion and skill of a trained person are required. As Harris and Webb have remarked, 'professionals do not create discretion; rather the inevitability of discretion creates the need for professionals'. (p. 4)

The reality of the situation, therefore, is that we have a complex situation in which regulation and professionalism are in a state of tension. However, this is far from saying that regulation negates professionalism. On the contrary, regulation sets the parameters in which professional judgements can be made. It neither removes the need for making such judgements nor makes them for us. Regulation therefore highlights the importance of professional accountability. In a context of multiple spheres of regulation, being able to account for our decisions and actions becomes even more important.

Davies (2000) writes of three forms of accountability:

- *Upwards*. This refers to accountability to our employers – our duty to abide by organisational policies and procedures, for example.
- *Downwards*. We are also accountable to our clientele. That is, we must remember that, while we may be employed by an organisation and have responsibilities to it, it is actually service users' interests that we should be addressing.
- *Sideways*. We are also part of a profession and have responsibilities to that profession – in terms of values, ethical requirements and quality standards, for example.

Exercise 2.5

Consider a small number of pieces of work that you are currently engaged in. For each of these, can you identify the lines of accountability in each of the three directions – that is, upwards, downwards and sideways?

If you are not currently directly involved in community care practice, see if you can find someone who is who is willing to talk to you about these issues.

It can be argued that the most important form of regulation is *self-regulation* – the commitment of professional practitioners to uphold professional values and standards. Without such self-regulation in the form of professional commitment, other forms of regulation can be at best only a partial safeguard.

Quality assurance

Are standards of practice high enough? How do we know? What mechanisms are in place to rectify the situation if standards fall below an acceptable level? These are the types of questions that form the basis of quality assurance. It is not enough to appoint what seem to be good people and then hope that their work will be of a sufficiently high standard. This is for the following reasons:

- People who appear to be competent, reliable workers may not actually be so. It is sadly the case that there are on record many examples of workers whose standards have been poor even though they managed to give the impression that they were highly competent and committed. What is perhaps even sadder is that there are also many people who have appeared to be working in an ethically sound way who, upon closer scrutiny, have been found to be highly abusive and exploitative (consider, for example, the institutional abuse of children in care – Waterhouse, 2000).
- Workers who are normally competent and reliable may function below par at certain times – as a result of stress (Thompson, 1999), grief (Thompson, 2002a) or other such potential disruptions to high-quality practice. We cannot assume that a competent worker with the best of intentions will function at acceptable levels at all times.
- There may be misunderstandings or a lack of awareness of what is necessary for high-quality practice. For example, someone who does not understand the value of needs led assessment and its importance may fall into the trap of oversimplifying the situation by assuming that, due to a lack of resources, a service-led assessment is all that is possible. That is, he or she may be labouring under the misapprehension that needs-led assessment is only valid when the resources are available to meet the identified needs, thus failing to appreciate the role of needs-led assessment in:
  (i) identifying unmet need and resource shortfall for planning and policy purposes; and
  (ii) forming the basis for more creative approaches to problem solving.

Clearly, then, there need to be mechanisms in place for ensuring that (i) standards of practice do not fall below an acceptable level; and (ii) if they do on occasion, the problems are rectified at the earliest opportunity.

In health care there is an important concept that has not yet been translated into a social work context, namely 'clinical governance'. The following passage from Rawaf and Powell (2001) explains it well:

Clinical governance is:
  a system through which all of the organisations in the National Health Service are accountable for continuously improving the quality of their clinical services and

ensuring high standards of patient care by creating a facilitative environment in which excellence will flourish. (Chief Medical Officer, 1999)

- It is basically a framework for the improvement of patient care through commitment to high standards of reflective practice, risk management and personal and team development.
- It is about providing the best possible clinical care for patients, identifying and avoiding areas of high risk in patient care, making the most effective use of available resources.
- It is about the individual clinical responsibilities of doctors, nurses and other health care staff and the collective responsibility of the team, service or organisation and the balance between them.
- It aims to put high-quality care at the heart of all decisions made, at whatever level, within the NHS. (p. 292)

We would suggest that there is much that community care workers can learn from this model, but it is unfortunately the case that we are a long way from such a systematic and focused approach. There is much that needs to be developed.

One of the most important bases of quality assurance is supervision. A major element of professional supervision is management accountability – that is, supervisors satisfying themselves that standards of practice are sufficiently high and that work efforts are appropriately targeted (Morrison, 2001; Thompson, 2002b). We should therefore not underestimate the vitally important role of high-quality regular supervision in quality assurance.

Exercise 2.6

Do you receive regular, high-quality supervision? If so, how can you build on this to make the most of it as a quality assurance mechanism? If not, what steps can you take to attempt to rectify or improve the situation? If you have other colleagues in the same boat, how can you work together to address the issues?

In addition to ongoing supervision as a quality assurance mechanism we also have broader processes, such as auditing. In this regard, the views of Adams (1998) on quality assurance are very significant. He points out that auditing is the term used by the Audit Commission to describe processes of checking that public money is being spent economically, efficiently and effectively. He then goes on to draw an important distinction between conventional and progressive approaches:

Different approaches to auditing predominate: conventional, focusing on quality imposition or maintenance; and progressive, focusing on quality enhancement or maximisation.

The *conventional* approach fulfils more restricted financial goals and the managerialist requirement of controlling practice. It relies typically on a technical, tick-list approach. . . .

The *progressive* approach to audit attempts to engage with the complexity of professional practice – not least the difficulties of decision-making and, despite standards and checklists, the lack of a single answer to problems. This approach also takes on board possible structural features of this, rather than pathologising them. (pp. 145–6)

Adams is indicating that there is a danger that quality assurance can become narrow and proceduralised, failing to take account of the complexities of what Schön (1983) calls the 'swampy lowlands of practice'. It is therefore important that a critical approach to such matters is adopted so that we do not become bogged down in bureaucratic orthodoxy – once again a *professional* approach is called for.

In a later work (Adams, 2002), he describes four approaches to quality assurance in social work. These are:

- *Rectification of errors and shortcomings in quality* Here he is referring to inquiries and investigations undertaken when there is a serious breakdown in service quality or appropriateness. These can be very helpful in some respects but can also encourage an unhelpful 'blame culture', resulting in defensive practices.
- *Maintenance through standard setting and inspection* This refers back to the issues of regulation and inspection discussed above. Adams argues that, while the principle of inspection is a good one, it is not enough on its own to ensure quality.
- *Quality enhancements through audit and evaluation* As indicated above, audits, with their reliance on checklists and statistics, can become very narrow and proceduralised, while evaluation processes (although very underused in social work) can offer a much richer picture of quality and what needs to be done to enhance it.
- *Quality maximisation* Adams argues that organisations must be supportive of their staff (in preventing stress, for example) if they are to enhance quality as fully as possible. Our comments above about the importance of supervision would be very relevant here, although staff support needs to go beyond simply supervision.

The fourth of these approaches is, in our view, the one that holds most promise (in so far as it relates well to the clinical governance model discussed above), but it is perhaps also the most difficult to achieve.

Adams' work on quality assurance is carefully thought through and has much to commend it. In particular, we would support his view that:

- We cannot maximise quality through quality assurance alone, or through approaches based on imposing regulation, standardisation, or one based on problem rectification. It is difficult to envisage how regulating a system which is not working will improve it significantly. Such a system needs reforms outside the quality assurance process and, probably, more resources.

- We cannot maximise quality without empowering clients and workers, including managers as well as professionals. A de-skilled, demotivated, stressed, overworked workforce is not well placed to help other people.
- Professionals and managers will continue to have an uneasy, and potentially bumpy, relationship. The way to address potential conflicts between professional and managerial interests is for managers constantly to check out with social workers any implications for them of proposed new approaches to quality assurance. Likewise, practitioners have a responsibility to go beyond maintaining handed-down standards and to criticise approaches to quality. (p. 294)

In Part One we identified some key issues relating to the law and regulation aspects of community care. Our task now is to draw out some of the implications of these issues for day-to-day practice. We shall concentrate on six issues in particular:

1. Shifting emphases

Community care is part of a broader movement away from state provision of welfare services towards an emphasis on funding or brokering and regulating services. An important practice implication of this is the need to recognise that, while there is less emphasis these days on the direct provision of services, care management is none the less still a social work role (as discussed in Part One), with all that entails in terms of a commitment to problem solving, empowerment and social work values.

2. The legal context

While the NHSCCA is clearly the major piece of legislation when it comes to community care, we should also recognise that many other laws have a significant bearing on community care practice. We should therefore make sure that we do not focus too narrowly on the NHSCCA at the expense of other significant pieces of legislation.

3. Developments in law and policy

There are very many current policy developments that are very significant for community care, a clear indication of how the field is a rapidly developing one. No one is expected to be an expert in these many and varied changes, but there is, none the less, a clear need to keep abreast of at least the basic implications of each new initiative. A commitment to continuous professional development is therefore needed.

4. Regulation and professional accountability

There are various ways in which community care practice is regulated by appropriate bodies. However, this is no substitute for professional accountability. It is important to be aware of the requirements imposed on us by such bodies but also to go beyond them in making sure that we are not practising in ways that are contrary to legal or ethical mandates. Although extensive, regulatory mechanisms remain fairly basic and so good practice relies on *self*-regulation.

5. Quality assurance

Similarly, while there are various mechanisms in place to ensure basic quality standards are met and, where possible exceeded, these are far from sufficient in themselves and need to be supplemented by our own commitment to quality maximisation and the commitment of our organisation through, for example, supervision and staff support more broadly.

6. Equality assurance

Alongside quality assurance we also need to address equality assurance. That is, we need to make sure that our practice promotes equality and values diversity. Community care is a pressurised activity, but we have to make sure that we do not allow such pressures to lead us into losing sight of what we are trying to achieve and the values on which such work is based (see the discussion of systematic practice in Chapter 5). We shall return to this topic in Part Three.

When it comes to the knowledge base relating to law and regulation with regard to community care, we are clearly talking about not only a large and complex one, but also one that is changing and developing at quite a rate. We have therefore not attempted to provide anything resembling a comprehensive account of this knowledge base or its implications for practice, as that would be far too unrealistic. What we have presented, in its place, is what we hope you will find to be sufficient raw material to encourage further discussion, debate, study and learning. We hope that you will find our comments helpful in encouraging critically reflective practice in which you can combine your own knowledge, experience and understanding with the insights offered here to form the basis of high-quality, skilful and well-informed practice.

Chapter 8
Making Partnership Work

It is unfortunate that it has so often been the case that people working under the rubric of partnership have tended to oversimplify it and regard it simply as an expectation that those involved in delivering community care should 'work together'. Such an uncritical and oversimplified approach is far from adequate as a basis for understanding the complexities and subtleties of working in partnership. In order to begin to move away from such an unsophisticated approach, the remainder of this section will be devoted to exploring what is involved in the three dimensions of partnership as identified in Part One: working with service users, working with carers, and multidisciplinary collaboration. However, before we do that, we can usefully form a bridge between our earlier discussions of systematic practice and partnership. Consider, for example, how the three key questions of systematic practice can be addressed in the context of partnership working:

- *What are you trying to achieve?* This involves setting objectives. And, of course, this needs to be done *jointly*. It is unlikely that imposing your own definition of what needs to be achieved will be a successful strategy.
- *How are you going to achieve it?* Here there needs to be a shared process of deciding what needs to be done to meet the objectives identified. It may well be that, given the care manager's experience and expertise across a wide range of social situations, he or she may be in a much stronger position to comment on possible solutions or plans of action. However, this does not alter the fact that the client also has much to contribute. They will know their situation much better than you do, of course, and therefore need to be as fully involved in the process as possible.
- *How will you know when you have achieved it?* It is important to have a clear picture of what success looks like. That is, we need to be clear about how we will know whether or not we have achieved what we set out to. Again this needs to be done jointly. If your idea of what constitutes a successful outcome is different from the client's, then clearly, this is going to lead to difficulties. If there is a difference of opinion about how success or otherwise will be recognised, then it is important to negotiate a mutually acceptable way forward if possible.

Working with clients

An important concept to consider here is that of professionalism. Professionalism is a word that means different things to different people. However, what we need to recognise is that one well-established usage of the term is what we would call the elitist model of professionalism and is characterised by the notion that the professional knows best. According to this model, a professional care worker would be the person who has the expertise and the access to resources, and is therefore in the best position to decide what should happen. However, in recent years, this model has come to be quite strongly challenged (Thompson, 2001). It has been argued that more democratic partnership-based forms of professionalism are possible and indeed desirable. According to such a model, the professional would bring his or her expertise and access to resources but would not use these as a power play to get his or her own way, but rather to put on the negotiating table alongside the wishes, feelings and, of course, needs of the service user and any carers involved. Partnership-based professionalism is therefore premised on working closely with service users to establish an agreed definition of their needs and any problems that need to be resolved as well as a jointly agreed action plan for meeting those needs and solving those problems. One implication of this model is that assessment should be shared assessment. In this respect, the model has much in common with the exchange model of assessment.

The exchange model of assessment features in the work of Smale *et al.* (1993). This model is contrasted with the questioning and procedural models. The three models can be described in the following terms:

- *Questioning*. This model is based on the idea that the worker is an expert in people and their problems and needs. The assessment, based on this expertise, involves identifying need and deciding the best way to meet that need. This is very similar to the elitist model of assessment in which the worker is the expert who 'knows best'.
- *Procedural*. This type of assessment involves gathering information to establish whether the client meets identified eligibility criteria. It is primarily a means of rationing scarce resources.
- *Exchange*. This model is one based on partnership, in so far as it involves the worker facilitating the process by which worker and client jointly identify needs and explore ways of meeting such needs.

The exchange model is more fully explained in the following passage from Smale *et al.* (1993):

THE EXCHANGE MODEL
Assumes that people:

- are expert in themselves.

Assumes that the worker:

- has expertise in the **process** of problem solving with others;

- understands and shares perceptions of problems and their management;
- gets agreement about who will do what to support whom;
- takes responsibility for arriving at the optimum resolution of problems within the constraints of available resources and the willingness of participants to contribute. (p. 18)

The exchange model is clearly the best suited of the three when it comes to working in partnership. Using this model means that responsibility for the situation is neither wrested from clients nor dumped upon them. Rather, it is shared, and this is important for the following four reasons:

- It is consistent with the value or ethical principle of partnership and the law and policy base to which it relates.
- It can be a source of motivation and stimulation for service users.
- It can be a source of job satisfaction for the worker.
- It can minimise the risk of recriminations if things do not go according to plan or other such difficulties arise.

Such a model has a number of implications. First of all, as we noted above, it can be linked to systematic practice. An important part of systematic practice is what we like to refer to as 'setting out our stall'. This means making it clear to the service user what our role is and what he or she can expect from us. For example, it involves clarifying that we will be undertaking a needs-led assessment but that we cannot necessarily guarantee that the resources will be available to meet those needs.

Exercise 2.7

Consider your own approach to assessment. Which of the three models does it come closest to? If you are already using the exchange model, how can you develop your knowledge and skills in this area. If you are not using the exchange model, what changes would you need to make to your practice to move in that direction?

This model of partnership also raises issues relating to skills. An important skill here is that of being able to 'manage expectations'. This involves negotiation skills, in so far as what is required is the ability to make sure that the service user does not have unrealistic expectations of what the worker can provide or achieve. This is an important part of partnership because, without this, (at least) two sets of problems can arise. Unrealistic expectations can lead to unnecessary:

- disappointment and resentment when they are not met – and can even be a source of aggression or violence; and/or

- additional pressure which can contribute to stress. Indeed, unrealistic expectations are recognised as a potential source of considerable stress (Thompson *et al.*, 1996).

Practice Focus 2.4

When Lal visited Mr Webb, she was taken aback by how high his expectations of her were. He gave her a long list of problems and made it quite clear that he expected her to resolve all of these for him. Lal had not been doing the job for very long and felt quite overawed by this, almost intimidated in fact. She made copious notes and told Mr Webb she would make enquiries and come and visit him again soon. 'Make sure that you do', he said quite forcibly as she made for the door. She returned to her office quite distressed and wondering how she would manage this situation. Mr Webb had not exactly been rude or aggressive, but he had none the less left Lal feeling under immense pressure to resolve all of his difficulties. Lal raised the issue with her team manager who talked her through the idea of 'managing expectations' and taught her how to 'set out her stall'. The next day Lal went back to Mr Webb with renewed confidence, although still feeling a little bit shaky. She did her best to put into practice what she had been taught. Although her performance was far from perfect she came away from that visit much happier. Mr Webb was still being quite demanding, but she had begun to negotiate with him about what she could realistically achieve and what she could not. She knew it was going to be difficult to complete her work in this case but she felt much better equipped for the challenge once she understood the principles of managing expectations.

As we have acknowledged, in all of this we need to be clear and focused in what we are doing, and so this necessarily introduces the importance of communication skills. Many people would regard effective communication as the ability to get one's message across successfully – and effectively conveying what we are trying to say is certainly an important part of communication. However, we should be wary of relying on such an approach, as this tends to go against the grain of partnership working. A more appropriate view of communication from a partnership perspective is that it involves a two-way process, not only getting our message across effectively, but also taking on board what the other person (or persons) is seeking to convey to us. Active listening skills, then, are very important components of effective communication (Thompson, 2003b).

An important means of understanding this is what philosophers refer to as phenomenology. Literally, phenomenology means the study of perception. It is concerned with how we use our senses to perceive, and thus make sense of, the world. It is very closely concerned with matters of perception, interpretation and understanding. A phenomenological approach to communication is one which emphasises the need to understand other people's perspectives or points of view. That is, we will find it difficult to communicate effectively with someone (let alone to enter into a meaningful partnership) if we are not able to understand how they see the world or at least how they see a particular situation they are trying to deal with. What is needed, then, is the ability to put ourselves in the service user's shoes, as it were, so that we can appreciate their concerns, their wishes and feelings and their overall approach to the situation. If we do not understand what the situation means to them, we will be in a very weak position when it comes to trying to resolve any difficulties associated with that situation.

This is closely linked to the idea of 'empathy'. While 'sympathy' refers to sharing the feelings of another person (for example, being sad because someone else is sad), 'empathy' refers to the ability to recognise another person's feelings without necessarily sharing those feelings. Sympathy can be very problematic, in so far as it can quickly lead to emotional overload and feeling overwhelmed by our work. Empathy, by contrast, can be very valuable in enabling us to understand the person or persons we are trying to help and thus be a significant aid when it comes to developing a phenomenological approach in which we are able to take account of people's perspectives, their wishes and their feelings.

What is also important in relation to partnership with service users is the significance of language use. Successful partnership work involves developing effective working relationships, and so we have to be careful to avoid language that undermines the development of such relationships. For example, we should ensure that we do not rely on any forms of language which are discriminatory, oppressive or patronising in any way. For example, in working with an elderly person, we should not assume without checking that he or she is happy to be referred to by first name only. Many of today's older people were brought up in an era when it was respectful to address people by title and surname, at least until you were on a much firmer footing in terms of a friendly relationship. What is seen as a friendly form of language by a younger person may therefore, in certain circumstances, be regarded as a disrespectful form of language by an older person.

Similarly, we should ensure that we avoid the inappropriate use of technical jargon. While jargon may be a useful shorthand for communicating with fellow professionals, it can act as a significant barrier when used with service users who may feel alienated by language that either they do not understand at all or which they may understand but which they associate closely with the professional perspective of the situation rather than their own. This does not mean that we should talk down to people, but it does mean that we should be careful not to allow inappropriate forms of language to slip into our conversation – and it is surprising just how easy it is for that to happen, especially when we are busy or distracted by other concerns (a common scenario in community care work, of course).

Practice Focus 2.5

When Phil was coming to the end of his placement in the community care team, his practice teacher asked him to do a small-scale evaluation of the work he had undertaken. With the help and advice of an experienced colleague, Phil drew up a short questionnaire and asked a number of the clients and carers he had worked with if they would mind filling it in. Overall, he was very pleased with the results, as most people commented on how hard he had worked to help them and how committed he was to doing a good job. However, what concerned him greatly was that two people had commented very unfavourably on his use of language. One had said that he 'talks like a dictionary' and another had said that: 'the way he talks didn't make us feel comfortable'. Phil was not only disappointed to receive this feedback, he was also quite amazed, as he had not realised that there was any problem whatsoever with his use of language or his communication skills more broadly.

An important point to recognise is that we become so used to the language we use (because it is such an integral part of our identity and our relationship with the outside world) that we may not be aware of what particular forms of language we are using or the impact it might be having. This presents a significant challenge in terms of developing increased levels of self-awareness (Thompson, 2002b).

Working with carers

Perhaps the first point to emphasise in terms of working in partnership with carers is that much, if not all, of what has been said in relation to working in partnership with service users can also be seen to apply here. In addition, of course, there are a number of other issues that need to be considered more specifically in the context of seeking to support carers in the important work that they undertake.

One very important point to emphasise is the central or primary role of carers in community care. While professionals from various disciplines clearly have a very important role to play, this is quite small by comparison with the huge amount of work undertaken by informal carers, such as relatives, friends and neighbours. As Finch and Groves (1983) pointed out a long time ago, community care is primarily care by the family. One implication of this is that professionals have a role to play in supporting carers as effectively as possible if community care is to be a successful venture. This raises important issues about partnership, as it means that the role of the care manager involves working in partnership with carers to support them – for example, by removing any possible obstacles to their ability to provide care. Sometimes the pressures that carers are under can contribute to what may be regarded as unacceptable behaviour – for example, abusive comments to the care manager. This can be a severe test of partnership, but here it is important to return to social work values, particularly in terms of unconditional positive regard (Rogers, 1961). This means that we have to provide whatever support is required (within reasonable parameters), regardless of how we may feel towards carers. This does not mean that they are given a licence to abuse, but it does mean that supporting carers can be a very complex and difficult matter, and is not simply a matter of providing services from a limited budget.

Practice Focus 2.6

Lisa had known Mr and Mrs Kingsley for some time and had been involved periodically when particular difficulties arose. However, when she received a phone call from the community nurse to indicate that the situation had deteriorated markedly, she needed to become involved more fully. Mrs Kingsley's problems had intensified in the past few weeks and Mr Kingsley, who was her primary carer, was under immense strain. When Lisa went to visit, she was not prepared for what she found. Mr Kingsley became very abusive towards her, and, among other things, told her that she was a waste of space and had never been any help to them. Initially Lisa was quite distraught by this and felt tempted to respond to his tirade defensively. However, she managed to 'bite her lip' and to restrain herself. She kept telling herself that caring can be a very stressful responsibility and that, while she could not condone Mr Kingsley's very offensive outburst, she could at least understand it. She therefore sought to work positively with him in supporting him through these difficult times. She knew she would find this difficult to do, but she reminded herself that her difficulties in dealing with the situation would be nothing by comparison with Mr Kingsley's.

Another social work value which is very relevant here is that of empowerment. A common scenario encountered in community care is overstretched carers finding it very difficult to cope with their caring duties. It is a very easy mistake to make to replicate the carer-cared for relationship by becoming a source of support to the carer in such a way which may create dependency. The principle of empowerment can be seen to apply to carers just as much as it does to service users, in the sense that it involves supporting them in gaining greater control over their lives. This means helping them to become aware of what obstacles there may be to their providing care and seeking, through a process of problem solving, to address any such barriers as far as is reasonably practicable. For example, feelings of guilt can have a major demoralising effect. This echoes the comments made in Chapter 1 about the importance of care management going beyond a simple process of basic assessment followed by the rationing of scarce resources. If we are to enable carers to play as full a role as possible in supporting vulnerable people with community care needs, we need to adopt a more sophisticated holistic approach that engages with the complexities of the demands they face and the subtle dynamics that can contribute so powerfully to the outcome of particular situations.

We noted earlier that shared assessment is part and parcel of partnership. In relation to carers, this has a twofold meaning. On the one hand, carers need to be involved in assessment in relation to service users, as it is likely that they will have an important contribution to make in terms of understanding the complexities of the situation. However, in addition to this, there are issues around assessing the carer's needs and ensuring that the whole community care package does not collapse because carers are not given adequate support. Unfortunately, this is often an area of practice which can be neglected, perhaps as a result of work overload and other related pressures.

The situation with regard to working in partnership with carers is therefore a complex one. On the one hand, carers are a mainstay of community care, often working very hard behind the scenes, perhaps never having any contact with a professional. On the other hand, carers and their needs can present a major challenge to care managers, in so far as a common task is that of supporting carers who are having particular difficulties. Carers may find it particularly difficult to cope at certain times for a variety of reasons, not least the following:

- The condition of the person being cared for deteriorates in general (as we noted in Practice Focus 2.6), thus increasing the demands on the carer.
- The condition of the person being cared for develops a new problem. For example, a person with dementia may start behaving in a very demanding or distressing way (wandering or aggression would be common examples).
- The carer experiences difficulties as a result of long-term caring responsibilities. That is, carers can quite simply become worn out.
- The carer experiences difficulties perhaps indirectly related to their caring responsibilities. For example, the strain of a caring relationship may be a contributory factor in the breakdown of the carer's marriage, and this breakdown can, in turn, become a major additional source of pressure for the carer.
- The carer experiences difficulties unconnected with the caring role (for example, a major bereavement), but which none the less add significantly to the pressures faced and/or undermine significantly the carer's ability to cope.

It should be clear, then, that this is a complex area, fraught with a number of difficulties and sensitive issues. We should therefore be wary of the common tendency to adopt an oversimplified approach to these issues which presents working with carers as being primarily about offering a bland combination of reassurance and respite.

Exercise 2.8

How would you describe your approach to working with carers? Is it consistent with the principle of partnership, as discussed earlier in this chapter? What steps can you take to strengthen partnership work with carers?˙

Multidisciplinary collaboration

The importance of multidisciplinary collaboration is increasingly being recognised – for example, in terms of the government's emphasis on a seamless service between health and social care provision (Chiu, 2001). In some ways, this is part of the government's 'third way', as discussed earlier (see Sullivan and Skelcher, 2002). This agenda has arisen largely because it has been recognised in a number of cases that conflicts of values, aims and roles can lead to major problems when professionals from different disciplines are required to work together on particular projects. It is perhaps naïve to expect that workers from diverse backgrounds can work effectively together without efforts being made to establish protocols for doing so.

The challenge of effective multidisciplinary partnership relies heavily on the effectiveness of the negotiation skills of those involved. Again, it is naïve to expect that people from such diverse backgrounds will be able to simply arrive at a consensus on which to base a way forward. The conflicting interests involved are bound to introduce the need for negotiation. Community care work can therefore be seen to rely on the development of a reasonably high level of negotiation skills.

Practice Focus 2.7

Ashok became very frustrated when he attended a multidisciplinary meeting to discuss plans for the establishment of a rapid response team. He could see that people from different agencies were pulling in different directions and no-one seemed to be making the effort to establish common ground. He decided that, before the next meeting in three weeks' time, he would see if he could spare the time to speak to some of the participants on a one-to-one basis. He was hoping that he could use his negotiation skills to establish some possible ways forward so that the next meeting could be much more fruitful and far more geared towards effective partnership.

The ability to negotiate is not simply a matter of being prepared to compromise or 'split the difference'. That would be a gross oversimplification of what is involved in the highly skilled processes of negotiation. The skills involved include:

- *Communication*. These can be broken down further into:
  - Getting one's message across effectively – conveying information appropriately.
  - Active listening – being able to 'engage' the other party or parties.
  - 'Reading' body language – being able to recognise and interpret successfully other people's non-verbal communication.
  - Appropriate use of body language – making sure that our own body language reinforces the message we are trying to put across rather than undermines or contradicts it.
- *Keeping a clear focus*. It is very easy in the pressure of a situation involving negotiation for us to lose our focus and to get drawn into other issues (petty squabbles, for example). It is therefore important that we are able to learn the lessons of systematic practice and to be able to maintain our focus despite the distractions that can arise in a negotiation situation.
- *Analytical skills*. We can easily find ourselves in complex situations, with a lot of information to absorb and make sense of. It is therefore important that we are able to *analyse* – that is, to identify significant patterns and interrelationships, so that we are able to make sense of the complexities rather than get lost in them.
- *Maintain our values*. Our values are a major influence on our actions. However, at times, particularly pressurised times, we run the risk of losing sight of our values and acting in a way that is inconsistent with them. For example, we may have a very strong commitment to fairness, but may be tempted to act quite unfairly in a negotiation situation if this may secure us a more favourable outcome from the negotiation. It is sometimes the case that the very powerful dynamics of a negotiation situation can draw us into adopting a 'win-lose' mentality (trying to get our own way at the other party's expense), rather than seeking a 'win-win' situation (an outcome that all parties are happy with).
- *Assertiveness*. Assertiveness skills are widely taught these days (but perhaps still not as widely as they should be). The process of assertion involves trying to achieve outcomes that involve all parties respecting one another's position and seeking mutually acceptable outcomes, rather than one party trying to manipulate or force the other party into a position of weakness or defeat. This has much in common with what is generally referred to as 'principled negotiation', a point to which we shall return below.
- *Building trust*. Where trust is not present, neither is effective partnership working. We must do all we reasonably can to build trust – for example, by being honest and open in our communications, by keeping our promises and fulfilling our commitments and by making sure that we act in ways that are, as far as possible, in everyone's interests, not just our own.

One important point to recognise in relation to negotiation is that it is not simply a matter of 'resolving' differences. Indeed, as we have argued previously, using difference positively is an important part of partnership working:

> This means regarding differences between groups of people as a source of strength. Differences should be seen as an aspect of the richness of diversity, rather than as a set of problems or difficulties. Partnership is not about everyone trying to be the same, but rather taking the opportunity to learn from each other and benefit from our differences. (Thompson and Thompson, 2002, p. 76)

By definition, negotiation situations are those where there are differences of interest between the respective parties. Traditional approaches to negotiation have tended to veer towards trying to eliminate these differences through either a process of compromise, or one of head-to-head conflict to try to force the other party to back down, or a mixture of the two. A more modern and more constructive approach is that of 'principled negotiation'. This involves taking a broader view of the situation, considering the respective interests of the parties involved and trying to find a creative way forward which will enable all parties to feel reasonably satisfied with the outcome (hence the link with assertiveness). For a discussion of principled negotiation, see Chapter 16 of Thompson (2002a).

Negotiation, then, does not necessarily involve 'doing battle' and can be a very constructive process of benefit to all concerned. We therefore need to avoid the destructive extremes of (i) regarding negotiation as a form of guerilla warfare; and (ii) avoiding negotiation altogether, for fear of 'rocking the boat' or being seen as 'difficult'. In between these two unhelpful extremes is the much healthier area of constructive, principled negotiation – a vitally important part of successful partnership working.

Linked to the idea of negotiation is the occasional need for conflict resolution skills. While negotiation skills can be useful for trying to make sure that conflicts of interest do not develop into out and out conflict, conflict resolution skills can be drawn upon when things start to go wrong, when tensions develop to such a level that steps need to be taken to defuse a situation. If we wish to promote effective multidisciplinary collaboration in a community care context, we clearly need to be open to developing our skills in this area. However, as these skills are very valuable in human services work in general, it should not be seen as a major undertaking, in the sense that a sound foundation should already be in place.

Conflict resolution skills are similar to negotiation skills, but are used in situations where there is not only a conflict of interest, but also a conflict of position which is proving problematic – a dispute that needs to be resolved, for example, or perhaps a relationship that is so strained that it is breaking down (or has broken down).

To attempt to resolve such a conflict involves seeking to understand the position of all parties (including the feelings that have been generated in the process of the development of the conflict) in order to explore the potential ways forward. If this is being undertaken by a neutral third party (a mediator or 'alternative dispute resolution' specialist, for example), the need to remain objective and not take sides is paramount. However, where it is one or more parties within the dispute situation who are trying to work out the conflict, then this becomes much more difficult.

Such situations can be a real challenge to our ability to work together. What can be very helpful is to revisit the basis of the partnership, to reaffirm its purpose, the shared goals and commitments, and use this as a foundation on which to build.

Whatever happens in such conflict situations, one vitally important thing to remember is that the interests of service users and carers and the overall quality of services provided must remain a primary consideration above and beyond any multidisciplinary conflicts that may arise.

At times, the difficulties may be so considerable and the need to address them so great that it becomes necessary to draw upon the services of a neutral third party, such as a mediator or an external facilitator skilled and experienced in helping teams or other groups address conflicts constructively to enable progress to be made.

Practice Focus 2.8

The situation became so tense in the multidisciplinary team that it seemed that it was only a matter of time before people lost their tempers with one another. Sue, the team manager, was at the end of her tether. She kept reminding colleagues of the importance of working together and of keeping a primary focus on service users' needs, but this seemed to fall on stony ground, such was the depth of bad feeling that had developed.

After discussing the situation with her line manager, a decision was made to hold a team-building day and to engage an external facilitator to try to assist the team in airing the difficulties and seeking a positive resolution.

The actual day of team building was a very difficult one for all concerned, and no-one had been looking forward to it. However, the facilitator was very skilled and experienced and managed to help the team identify three key areas of conflict. The day itself resolved one of those areas and enabled the team to identify an action plan for dealing with the other two. Sue was delighted with the progress made and felt much more confident about helping the team members to work effectively together on a day-to-day basis.

Of course, as we have noted, successful negotiation and conflict resolution rely on a fairly highly developed level of communication skills. The basic skills involved in communication are in abundance in human services but it is likely that they will need to be developed to a more advanced level if we are to be successful in promoting multidisciplinary working. One particularly important subset of communication skills is that associated with 'cross-cultural' communication. This term is generally used in relation to communication across national or ethnic cultures (Guirdham, 1999). However, the same term can also apply to communications which take place across professional and organisational cultures, as differences between such cultures can be just as much of a barrier to communication as they are between other types of culture. Such cross-cultural communication involves being able to appreciate the perspective of the other party from their cultural vantage point while also being able to convey one's own cultural position in return. This returns us to the topic of phenomenology and its emphasis on perception, interpretation and meaning. Such effective cross-cultural communication is clearly a highly skilled undertaking. However, its importance as a basis for effective multidisciplinary partnership cannot be underestimated.

Once again, the dangers of work overload need to be identified here, as an excess of such work pressures can lead people to focus primarily, if not exclusively, on their own professional domain and to fail to take account of the important issues arising from partners in other professional groupings. This can lead to a vicious circle in which work pressures lead to a failure to achieve satisfactory multidisciplinary working which, in turn, create further work pressures due to the difficulties arising from the failure of partnership.

Exercise 2.9

What barriers to effective multidisciplinary collaboration are you able to identify? What steps do you feel can be taken to address these issues? Are there other steps you (and your colleagues) could take to promote partnership in these areas?

It is important to recognise that multidisciplinary partnership, while an important goal to achieve, is not necessarily an easy one to attain. There can be a number of ways in which such collaboration can break down or fail to get off the ground. Weinsteln (1998) identifies the following barriers:

Lack of shared aims and goals
Different language/jargon
Conflicting values/ethics/attitudes
Different cultures
Status differences – minority dominate
Race and gender issues – lack of involvement and participation by key members
Lack of knowledge about each other's roles
Lack of clarity about tasks and responsibility
Power struggles

Unexpressed conflict leading to poor communication and distrust
Inability/unwillingness to share
Lack of knowledge about group/organisational dynamics
Lack of self-awareness
Rigid and narrow view of remit
Lack of clarity about interagency procedures and decision-making processes
Size of team too large for successful interaction (cited in Baxter and Toon, 2001, p. 276).

These are large and complex issues, and certainly not ones we can satisfactorily address in the space available to us here. However, forewarned is forearmed. If we know that these are likely pitfalls, then we can at least begin to take the necessary steps to avoid them.

Multidisciplinary collaboration is, of course, not a new idea. It has been accepted as part of good practice for quite some considerable time. However, these days it has an extra degree of emphasis, partly because of the governmental emphasis on 'joined up working' and partly because of developments in the knowledge and values bases of social work which now set much greater store by the importance of 'working together'.

This is partly due to the difficult lessons that have had to be learned in child protection about the disastrous consequences that can arise as a result of the failure of multiagency systems to work. Of course, there is still a long way to go in developing multidisciplinary partnership in child protection, as in any other area of social welfare practice. It is to be hoped that the progress that has been made in recent years, in both child protection and community care, can be sustained and built upon.

In summary, we can identify five key issues relating to working in partnership:

1. The importance of partnership

In recent years we have been steadily moving away from the traditional approach based on the idea that the professional knows best, and that he or she is therefore best placed to decide what the problems are and what the possible solutions are. This is gradually being replaced by a partnership-based approach in which workers are expected to use their skills to engage with service users and carers (and indeed others involved in the process) in order to establish as far as possible a shared assessment of what problems need to be addressed and how best to address them. This is, of course, more easily said than done in many cases – and this is the real challenge of partnership. However, we do at least know that a partnership-based approach is far more likely to be effective than one based on 'diagnosing' the problem and 'prescribing' the required 'treatment' to rectify the situation.

2. Working in partnership with clients

A key practice implication here is the ability to put ourselves in the other person's shoes (that is, to adopt a phenomenological approach). This involves being able to understand the situation being dealt with from the point of view of the service user, so that we are better able to appreciate their concerns, their wishes and feelings, and therefore their needs. For example, it is no coincidence that Sue Thompson's training manual on working with older people is entitled *From Where I'm Sitting*. It deliberately sets out to emphasise the importance of understanding the older person's point of view. And, of course, it is not only to older people that this concept applies. The Disabled People's Movement has for many years criticised social work practice with disabled people for being patronising and dispempowering, for not taking account of the disabled person's point of view (see, for example, Oliver and Sapey, 1999).

3. Working in partnership with carers

Again a phenomenological approach has significant implications for practice. If we are to take seriously the matter of working in partnership with carers, then we have to be able to understand each situation we deal with from their perspective. This has implications in terms of skills (particularly listening skills), but it is also significant in terms of values. That is, if we are to be successful in this regard, then we must value carers for the crucially important role they play. What we must not do, of course, is take carers for granted. At face value, this sounds a self-evident point to make. However, we have to be realistic and accept that, in the pressure of a busy workload and competing demands on our time, it is an easy mistake to make to take carers for granted rather than work in partnership with them.

4. Multidisciplinary collaboration

Increasingly there is an emphasis on multiagency partnership and a 'seamless service'. This means that working with individual service users and their carers cannot be done in isolation. We have to recognise that the time, effort and energy it takes to develop successful multiagency partnerships are a worthwhile investment, given the importance of ensuring that professionals from different backgrounds work towards common goals rather than pulling apart or getting in each other's way. Of course, developing such positive working relationships is no easy task, but the important point to realise here is that the skills involved in such work are important ones to develop and build upon as far as we reasonably can.

5. Negotiation and conflict resolution

These too are important skills to develop. It is important to be able to move away from simplistic models of care management which see the process as one of identifying need and rationing resources. Of course, the reality is far more complex and involves a wide-ranging set of skills, including the skills necessary to deal with situations involving actual or potential conflicts of interest (negotiation) and those where conflict has reached the point of a dispute or the actual or potential breakdown of working relationships (conflict resolution). These are related sets of skills, but both are important in making sure that partnership working is more than a rhetorical statement and actually has some basis in reality. Successful community care practice involves the ability to link up well with others involved in the complex multidisciplinary network, to handle conflict constructively and to maximise the positive potential across professional boundaries.

The idea of 'partnership' has become something of a buzzword in recent years. However, it is a deceptive word. It does not simply mean working alongside other people, but rather *how* we work alongside others. It is quite a complex notion, and one that deserves more detailed and critical analysis than it often achieves. In these days of glib sound bites and easy answers we have to be careful that we do not allow ourselves to use important terms like partnership without a clear understanding of what they mean and how they relate to the work we undertake. This chapter has, we hope, provided a sound foundation for an understanding of partnership which does justice to the complexity and importance of the term.

Of course, many will argue that partnership is not possible, that it is a pipe dream. They will argue that a lack of resources plus some inherent tensions in the worker-client relationship will make partnership an unrealistic goal to aim for. However, this is to fail to understand the nature and significance of partnership. There will inevitably be difficulties at times in developing effective partnerships, and it would be naïve not to recognise that there are very clear limitations when it comes to partnership working. We have to be *realistic* in approaching partnership issues. However, we would wish to make a very clear and firm distinction between realism and defeatism. In highly pressurised times it is very easy to allow negativism to creep in and to equate realism with defeatism. The basic truth is that a realistic approach is one that recognises that there will be obstacles, tensions, limitations and difficulties, but also acknowledges that there will be excellent potential for building positive working relationships with service users and carers and forming fruitful alliances with colleagues across a range of agencies and professional groups. If we allow cynicism and defeatism to replace realism, then we do some very vulnerable people a considerable disservice as we deny them the possibility of positive and empowering change.

Conclusion

Part Two has covered a wide range of issues, all of which have an important bearing on care management. It has by no means been comprehensive or exhaustive in its coverage. Therefore, when we take account of the fact that the complex issues explored here are only a sample of the full range of relevant issues that can be seen to apply, we can perhaps realise just how complex and demanding an undertaking care management is.

Part Two has provided a general introduction to some important practice issues and has therefore played a role in establishing a foundation for good practice. We are now ready to proceed to Part Three where we build on the work done in the first two parts of the book by exploring how community care can play a part in promoting anti-discriminatory practice.

Part Three: Tackling Discrimination and Oppression

Introduction

In this part of the book we look at how we can try to ensure that community care practice challenges discrimination and oppression. We begin, in Chapter 9, by looking at reflective practice and how it is an important foundation for building *emancipatory* practice – that is, forms of practice which not only avoid reinforcing discrimination, but also actually play a part in empowering people so that they are better equipped to take control of their lives by escaping the restrictions of stereotyping and other such discriminatory processes.

In Chapter 10 our focus switches to 'equality assurance', which refers to the steps we can take to ensure that practice takes account of the need to promote equality and to value diversity. This builds on our earlier discussions of the importance of quality assurance. We examine how various forms of discrimination (racism and sexism and so on) feature in community care work and how we can try to make sure that our practice makes a positive contribution to tackling discrimination and oppression.

Chapter 9
Reflective Practice

Reflective practice is not just a simple process of 'reflecting on' practice, as if thinking about our work will somehow automatically make us more effective workers. Rather, it is a complex concept that involves quite a significant departure from traditional ways of thinking about theory and professional practice, as we shall see below.

Reflective practice is an approach to professional learning and practice which owes much to the work of the educational theorist, Donald Schön (1983, 1987, 1992). Schön distinguished between the 'high ground' of theory and research (where a clear view of patterns and interconnections is more easily achieved) and the 'swampy lowlands' of practice where situations are messy and indeterminate and not easily solved by formula solutions. Reflective practice involves trying to incorporate the insights from the high ground into the complex reality of the swampy lowlands – to get the best of both worlds: practice wisdom/experience plus the lessons to be learned from theory and research. As Thompson (2002b) comments:

> Schön described the world of theory and research as the 'high ground', likening it to a hill that gives a clear overview of the landscape below. From here it is relatively easy to develop a picture of what is going on below – to see links, connections, patterns, blockages and so on. However, this can be quite different from the much messier, more complex and uncertain world of actual practice which he described as 'the swampy lowlands'. What is called for, then, is the ability to remember and draw upon the insights offered by the high ground while actually navigating the much more difficult terrain of actual practice. The insights of the high ground are of relatively little use if we ignore them in practice and a form of practice that cannot see further than the next few metres of bog is also not likely to be of much value! Integration through reflection is the key.

Reflective practice involves replacing the traditional idea of 'applying theory to practice' (a one-way process) with the integration of theory and practice (a two-way process). Insights from theory and research should guide and inform practice, but practice should test and help develop theory.

In order to understand this more fully it is important to be aware of the distinction between reflection-in-action and reflection-on-action. The process of reflection involves both reflection-*in*-action (thinking on our feet – tailoring the professional knowledge base to suit the specific circumstances at the time) and reflection-*on*-action (taking time afterwards to see what can be learned from the experience). The basic idea is that we can use the insights we gain from reflection-on-action to improve our skills in reflection-in-action. If we are not aware of a skill we have developed, then we will not be in a position to develop it further. Therefore, among the potential benefits of reflection-in-action is the additional learning that we can gain from the higher level of self-awareness that a reflective approach facilitates. For example, we develop non-verbal communication skills as part of growing up, but to be able to use them at an advanced level (in averting aggression, perhaps), we need to develop a greater awareness of them so that we can build on our strengths. Reflection-on-action can play a very significant role in helping us to develop that greater level of awareness.

Similarly, much of the professional knowledge base we draw on is 'submerged', in the sense that we generally do not appreciate how much our actions and decisions are influenced by our understanding of human development, interpersonal dynamics, the operation of power in society and so on, as well as an understanding of law and policy and ethics. Reflective practice involves 'surfacing' this knowledge (making it explicit) so that we can make the best use of it, build on it, use it to explain and/or justify our actions, and so on. This can be done on an individual basis as part of taking responsibility for our own learning, or through supervision, a mentoring relationship or indeed training.

A basic principle of reflective practice is the recognition of the importance of avoiding relying on 'routinised practice' – that is, using routines in inappropriate situations. Routines can be very helpful, efficient responses to many situations. However, a routine response to a non-routine situation is potentially a very dangerous course of action (Thompson, 2000a). It is therefore an important reflective practice skill to be able to distinguish between those situations that can be safely dealt with on a routine basis and those that cannot. Getting this wrong can lead to either a significant waste of time and energy (failing to adopt an efficient routine approach to situations where it is safe and appropriate to do so) or engaging in highly dangerous forms of practice (adopting a routine approach in situations which are far too complex or out of the ordinary for such a course of action to be safe or effective).

What adds extra weight to the importance of reflective approaches to practice is that there is a strong relationship between reflective practice and anti-discriminatory forms of practice, in so far as both involve:

- *Raising awareness:* Reflective practice involves going beyond everyday understandings of events and interactions to develop a more insightful approach, while anti-discriminatory practice involves becoming more aware of discriminatory processes that commonly take place in society.
- *Challenging assumptions and stereotypes:* Discrimination is not simply a matter of personal prejudice. It also involves a reliance on discriminatory assumptions and stereotypes, and so attempts to develop anti-discrimina-

tory practice need to include a willingness to question such assumptions (Thompson, 2001). Reflective practice also involves questioning assumptions and avoiding unthinking responses.

- *Adopting a critical perspective:* Many approaches to social work can be criticised for being 'reductionist' – that is, reducing complex, multi-level phenomena to simplistic, single-level explanations. A critical perspective is one which avoids reductionism and takes account of the complexities involved.

Practice Focus 3.1

Sandra returned to the office after a very difficult morning and felt drained after her experience. She had been to visit Steven, a 25-year-old man with cerebral palsy, to discuss his desire to move out of the family home. His mother and stepfather had been present, as too had his fiancée. They all had their own views on the wisdom and feasibility of Steven's plans. Sandra had felt like she was being pulled in several different directions, as each person voiced their anxieties and tried to convince her that she should be 'on their side'. Back in the office she reviewed the case but could see no way forward, as it seemed she was being expected to be all things to all people. Feeling ineffective in her role she discussed the situation with her colleague, who suggested she let her anxiety subside a little before revisiting the situation with a fresh perspective. With a clearer head Sandra realised that she had been neglecting to consider the wider family context which usually informed her practice and, instead, had been seeing individuals but not the dynamics between them. Having reminded herself of her knowledge base in this area she was soon able to analyse the family situation and plan for future work with them that would take these tensions into account. She realised that her experience had shown her that this was usually an effective approach and that neglecting interpersonal dynamics and the power issues associated with them could easily lead to discriminatory outcomes.

In order to promote emancipatory forms of practice which challenge discrimination and oppression, it is therefore clearly necessary to promote reflective practice. There are various strategies that can be used to do this. These include:

- *Asking 'why?'* This is an important means of trying to understand people's reasoning, although this has to be done carefully and sensitively if it is not to be experienced as threatening.
- *Exploring options.* There is rarely, if ever, a single solution to a particular problem. It is therefore important to explore a range of options if we are to avoid the tramlines of routinised practice. This is particularly relevant to care management where a routinised, service oriented approach is so easy to slip into.

- *Being creative.* It is understandable that the pressure of work can at times lead people into adopting a narrow approach. However, this is very much a temptation to resist as creative thinking is an important part of effective problem-solving – which is an important part of meeting people's needs.
- *Using frameworks of understanding.* There are numerous tools or frameworks of understanding that can be used to help make sense of complex situations and plot a route through them. One such example is SWOT analysis which involves identifying the **S**trengths, **W**eaknesses, **O**pportunities and **T**hreats of a particular situation (see Thompson and Bates, 1998). Such frameworks can be useful in gaining insights into a situation which would not normally be apparent to us.

Although there are such ways of promoting reflective practice, we also need to recognise that there are likely to be obstacles to reflective practice (for example, other people's negative or defeatist attitudes). It is important that we recognise this and take the necessary steps to avoid or remove these barriers.

Perhaps the greatest barrier to reflective practice is the (false) assumption that busy people do not have time for reflection. What this assumption fails to take into account is that, by investing time in creating 'windows for reflection', we will save time and energy in the long run. It is a fallacy to think that we do not have time for reflection. It is a considerable false economy to attempt to save time by omitting time for reflection from our busy schedules, as a reflective approach to practice is likely to be far more effective, to lead to far fewer mistakes and dead ends, and to be a source of motivation and job satisfaction.

Exercise 3.1

What opportunities do you get to reflect on your practice to ensure quality and to learn from your experience? If such opportunities are limited, what can you do (personally and collectively with colleagues) to create such opportunities?

Chapter 10
Equality Assurance

The development of anti-discriminatory practice has drawn attention to the fact that we need to develop not only quality assurance, but also equality assurance. That is, we need to ensure that issues of equality and diversity are not lost in the welter of issues that need to be addressed in the contemporary community care arena. We shall explore how issues of race, gender, class, age and disability need to be addressed in the context of community care.

Race and ethnicity

Over the years there has been considerable criticism of social work for failing to address issues of culture and ethnicity and to develop an adequate anti-racist approach. Community care has not been immune from these criticisms. As Ahmad and Atkin (1996a) comment:

> community service provision often ignores the needs of black and minority ethnic groups. For example, structural barriers to access are not taken into account . . . in the organization of services. Often service managers will say that services are 'open to all' regardless of ethnic background. Yet racial inequalities and poverty disadvantage minority ethnic people and can create additional barriers to gaining service support; and the dietary, linguistic and caring needs of ethnic minority communities are often disregarded because services are organized to white norms. (p. 3)

What has made the situation worse is that the approach to developing anti-racist practice has often been of a confrontational, if not actually aggressive, nature. This has had the effect in many places of creating a culture of fear in which people will often choose not to address the issues of race equality for fear of being labelled racist. Unfortunately, such a crude approach to complex and sensitive issues is highly counterproductive (Thompson, 2003a), but none the less, far from uncommon. Clearly, a much more sophisticated approach to race and culture is called for.

The implementation of the Race Relations (Amendment) Act 2000 should help us to go some way towards a more developed understanding of the issues, as this Act lays a duty on public authorities to take a more proactive approach to developing positive race relations (Hill, 2001). However, there is also the danger that, in their haste to put in place the necessary plans for complying with the Act, some public authorities may attempt to come up with simple solutions to complex problems and return us to the problems of a simplistic, reductionist approach to anti-racism based on an uncritical orthodoxy.

In order to ensure that equality issues are not neglected, it is important to include them in other quality assurance processes (supervision, for example), and to make sure that they are not dealt with superficially or tokenistically, or dismissed altogether ('There aren't many black people around here, so it's not an issue for me').

An important issue to address is that of institutional racism. As James and Baxter (2001) comment:

> It is important to emphasise that, although there will be incidences of personal racism, most people in the caring professions take seriously their obligation to treat all people with respect and would regard deliberate, overt discrimination as unprofessional behaviour. Institutional racism is far more common and more damning. It can happen:
> - by default, where the way things are done within organisations does not take account of the needs of black and ethnic minority people.
> - where the rules and regulations of the organisation apply equally to all, but they have the effect of excluding this section of the population while maintaining the privileged position of white people.
> - where people in positions of power base their decisions on assumptions and stereotypes. (pp. 264–5)

It is therefore important to strike a balance which avoids the destructive extremes. On the one hand we do not want an aggressive approach which works on the premise of assuming that white people are guilty of racism until proven innocent and which tends to be counterproductive, producing defensiveness and avoidance behaviour rather than learning and progress. On the other hand, we do not want an approach based on the notion that 'I am not racist and so this has got nothing to do with me'. Institutional racism shows that these matters are an issue for us all. Whether or not we are racist at a personal level, the fact remains that there is a great deal of evidence to show the prevalence of racism in our society and our organisations at cultural and structural levels (Thompson, 2001).

To ensure that our community care practice is consistent with anti-racist principles, then at the very least we must make sure that we:

- Consider carefully each client's cultural background – their needs, practices, beliefs and values – and how these contribute to a person's sense of identity.
- Take account of the existence and likely impact of racism – both direct and overt, on the one hand, and more subtle and hidden on the other – as very real aspects of black people's lives.
- Do not allow racist assumptions to influence our practice – recognising that assumptions about racial superiority/inferiority will for most of us have been part of our upbringing.

Practice Focus 3.2

Ben, a community care worker, had been asked to work with Nina, an elderly Asian woman who had been suffering from anxiety attacks after being burgled some months before. Aware that she had become isolated, Ben had suggested that she should try to become part of her local community again and Nina eventually agreed to make tentative steps towards doing so by attending a luncheon club in the centre of town. Having worked with many Asian people Ben felt that he was well able to anticipate her cultural needs and set about making arrangements for her to attend a club run by a local Asian organisation the following week. He visited Nina after her initial visit only to find that she was not willing to go again, as she had felt out of place. Surprised at this, since he had felt she would be amongst 'kindred spirits', he asked her to talk about her day. What emerged was that most of the other women had different life experiences, religious backgrounds and worldviews from her own. As a Christian from a remote part of India, she had found it difficult to find anyone with a common experience or viewpoint from which to establish a friendship and, as a consequence, had decided to withdraw again into her own home and her own company.

Ben realised that, although he had acted with the best of intentions, he needed to think things through further. He had tried to work in a culturally sensitive way, but had not appreciated the diversity that exists within cultural categories.

Gender

It has long been argued that community care is primarily care by the family and that care by the family is primarily care by women (Finch and Groves, 1983). What this helps us to realise is that gender is a very important dimension of community care. To attempt to practise community care without considering the significance of gender can therefore be seen as not only inadequate but also dangerous – in the sense that an uncritical approach could easily reinforce discrimination in this area.

One very important point to emphasise is the danger of relying on stereotypes – for example, the idea that it is 'natural' for women to provide care. Such a stereotypical assumption can be problematic in a number of ways:

- It places a huge burden on women, especially when they are unable to provide care or choose not to. The ideological weight given to the notion that caring is a female domain can lead to considerable feelings of guilt when women resist pressures to sacrifice their own needs in favour of caring for others.
- It means that assessment processes may be distorted – for example, when it is assumed that some men cannot cope unsupported *because* they are men. Resources may be allocated to men that would not be allocated to women in similar circumstances, thus introducing a further level of inequality.

Community care involves working with people who, for various reasons, are vulnerable and in need of support. This can mean that the individuals concerned rely heavily on the input of others, which can add an additional layer of vulnerability. For example, a person may be vulnerable to harm because of mental health problems, but may face an additional layer of vulnerability when their reliance on mental health services places them at risk of stigmatisation, dependency creation and so on. The work of staff involved in community care can therefore contribute to problems as well as solve them, if there is insufficient sensitivity to the potential to do harm.

The need for such sensitivity can also be extended to the gender dimensions of community care practice. If we do not take account of differences between men and women and the problems that arise from institutionalised patterns of sexism, then we run the risk of making the situation worse, of contributing to discrimination and oppression rather than challenging them through forms of practice that are emancipatory and empowering.

Indeed, empowerment is a key word. How can we expect to play a positive role in empowering people when we fail to incorporate into our practice an understanding of the complex and pervasive workings of gender inequality?

Exercise 3.2

Think carefully about your role in community care. In what ways does gender have a bearing on how you would carry out your role? In what ways can you envisage a failure to address gender issues leading to problems?

If you have the opportunity discuss these issues with one or more colleagues and compare notes. Do they have a different perspective from your own? If so, can you learn anything from that?

An important issue to consider here is the discussion in Part One of the dangers of a mechanistic approach to care management which focuses narrowly on bureaucratic processes of resource rationing and loses sight of the person. Gender is an important part of identity. Who we are and how we see ourselves will owe a great deal to how gender dynamics operate in our society and what meaning is attached to them at a cultural level. If we neglect gender as a consideration in our work because we have slipped into a mechanistic approach, we could find ourselves in a situation where our involvement becomes highly problematic, as illustrated in Practice Focus 3.3 below.

In order to ensure that our community care practice is consistent with the principles of anti-sexist practice, we must at the very least ensure that:

- We do not fall into the trap of relying on gender stereotypes, thus reinforcing discriminatory assumptions about women and men.

- We take account of gender differences and the significant role gender plays in shaping a person's identity – we cannot adopt a 'one size fits all' approach.
- We are sensitive to the dangers of others in involved in the process (colleagues, carers and even clients themselves) allowing gender inequalities to be reinforced in our assessment and/or intervention.

Practice Focus 3.3

Anwen had been brought up to respect herself as a person and to always strive to reach her potential. She took a pride in keeping her home clean and well decorated and, when her three children came along, she did her best to keep them well clothed, fed and socially stimulated. When they were old enough to go to school, she took on a part-time job and began evening classes, which she hoped would help her in her dream to become a mechanic. But Anwen was always tired and her support worker noticed that she was becoming increasingly irritable, with mood swings that had begun to affect how she cared for herself and her children. Anwen felt that she was failing at everything she tried. Her job made great demands on her mental and physical reserves and she was beginning to resent the demands her children made on her when she picked them up from school. Her house was becoming unkempt because she didn't have the energy to keep it tidy and this made her feel she was neglecting her 'duty'. And, because she was too tired to concentrate on her studies in the evening, she did not make the progress she was expecting to and felt she was letting herself down in that area too.

When the support worker realised how fragile her emotional state was, she felt that Anwen needed to make some changes. She suggested to her that she give up her job or her studying, or indeed both, so that she would have less to cope with. This only succeeded in making Anwen feel worse, as she felt she was being expected to comply with the expectation that she should only aspire to being a good housewife and mother.

Class

A person's class or 'socioeconomic position' can be very significant in relation to community care. It can have a bearing on, amongst other things:

- *Health and life expectancy*. The inequalities in health and mortality arising from class position have been well documented over the years – see, for example, Acheson (1998).
- *Housing*. Quality and suitability of housing are likely to be influenced by class and these in turn can be very relevant in shaping community care needs.
- *Financial security*. Whether a person has to rely on benefits or has a financial backup can, of course, make a huge difference to a person's life, their ability to withstand stress and to cope with adversity.

In undertaking a community care assessment, it is therefore important that we take account of class issues in general and poverty in particular, for, as Jones and Novak (1999) point out:

> As Richard Wilkinson's research (1996) convincingly shows, it is the relationship between poverty and wealth, and the degree of inequality within a particular society, that are the major determinants of not only physical but also of mental health. Poverty is a corrosive which acts not only through the effects of malnutrition and unhealthy living and working conditions, but also through those social relationships which depict the poor as worthless.
>
> Surviving poverty is thus not only a matter of trying to balance an inadequate budget. It is also having to deal with the social and psychological stress, with insecurity, social isolation and the often thinly disguised contempt of the more powerful. (pp. 25–26)

The same authors also write of the 'degradation of the human spirit' that poverty can bring about (p. 24). These, then, are not minor, peripheral issues, but rather core concerns that should alert us to the need to take very seriously matters relating to class, poverty and deprivation.

While it would clearly be unrealistic to expect community care workers to be in a position to eradicate poverty, we can at least be aware of its pervasiveness and its detrimental effects and do whatever we reasonably can to counter them – for example, putting clients in touch with welfare rights services where appropriate.

In order to ensure that we are not part of the problem when it comes to class, poverty and community care, we need at the very least to ensure that:

- We are aware of the significance of class in shaping people's lives and their sense of identity.
- We do not become judgemental about people based on stereotypes and discriminatory assumptions about poor people or people belonging to a particular class group.
- We take whatever reasonable steps we can to counteract the detrimental effects of poverty and deprivation in planning and/or delivering packages of care.

Practice Focus 3.4

Alex had been a keen gardener for all of his adult life and tried not to let the progressive muscle-wasting condition that had started in his fifties get in the way of it. Over the years he had adapted flowerbeds and equipment so that he could continue with the gardening that gave him such pleasure, prestige and identity. Everyone in his community respected his experience and came to him for advice. As his condition worsened, he confined himself to working in the greenhouse but, in time, even the journey there from his back door became too difficult. His neighbours noticed that he spent long hours gazing out at the garden and the decaying plants in the greenhouse. When he seemed to be sinking into self-neglect, his neighbours alerted the local authority and a community care worker, Joe, visited to assess the situation.

Joe was astute enough to recognise quite quickly that the likely key to Alex's recovery was facilitating access to his garden and, to this end, he offered to contact a number of companies who specialised in hard landscaping. He even recommended one which he had used himself when he was making changes to his own garden. But what Joe had failed to take into account was Alex's capacity to pay for such work. As someone with a regular salary, Joe had forgotten that not everyone was in the same affluent position as himself. If it been just a matter of money, Alex would have had the work done years before, but his present income barely covered his day-to-day living expenses. This was a salutary lesson for Joe, who had never been without disposable income since leaving school.

Exercise 3.3

In what ways could poverty influence the need for community care services? In what ways might you be able to address poverty issues through your work in community care? If possible, compare notes with one or more colleagues and see what you can learn from the different perspectives you encounter.

Age

Old age is not in itself a basis for needing community care services. However, many of the people who become recipients of such help are at an advanced age. Community care services therefore need to be aware of the dangers of ageist assumptions influencing practice in a detrimental way.

As with other forms of discrimination, a key issue in relation to ageism is stereotyping. Stereotypical assumptions about older people can lead to decisions being made for them without adequate consultation, based on what Midwinter (1990) refers to as 'postadulthood' – that is, the tendency to treat older people as if they have entered a second childhood. The rights and privileges that people acquire on reaching adulthood can be withdrawn on reaching old age if we allow ageist assumptions to hold sway.

The tendency to deny older people a voice is one that can be adopted by relatives or other carers. This can result in their putting community care staff under pressure to make decisions that they feel are in the elderly person's best interests. As we noted in our earlier discussion of risk assessment (see Chapter 4), it is only in limited circumstances that anyone has the right to make a decision affecting somebody without their permission. We must therefore make sure that we do not allow ageist assumptions to fall into the trap of responding inappropriately to pressure to act on the basis of 'we know best' and thereby silence the voice of the older person. Behaving in such a way in someone's 'best interests' does not, of course, make it acceptable.

Older people can face many problems but we have to make sure that we do not allow ageism to add to any difficulties they encounter. In particular, we need to make sure that:

- We do not rely on ageist stereotypes or other such discriminatory assumptions or fail to challenge others when they do so.
- We involve older people as fully as possible in the processes of assessment, care management and so on, focusing on empowerment rather than simply providing care (Thompson and Thompson, 2001).
- We take all reasonable steps to challenge ageism and to promote anti-ageist forms of practice.

Practice Focus 3.5

Irene had been working at the group home for a number of years. All four adults who shared the house had mild learning disabilities and Irene was one of the support workers who helped them in their aim to live as independently as possible in their community. Three of the residents were in their late forties but Doris was significantly older at 67 years. Irene had noticed that, when the others went on outings or to activities such as swimming, cycling or trekking in the countryside, Doris was usually excluded. At first she assumed that this was because Doris preferred not to go but, on seeing her so downhearted one evening, Irene asked her why she didn't participate. Doris told her that she generally wasn't asked and, assuming that the others didn't like her company, she hadn't pursued the matter for fear of having her feelings hurt. When Irene raised this matter with her line manager she was told that this had always been the case since Doris had arrived at the house two years ago, having been referred there by a team who worked with older people. Irene guessed that judgements made by support staff at the time, about Doris's competence and her right to independence and choice, could well have been influenced by ageist assumptions about what older people can and should expect. She wondered whether a pattern had been set which allowed the negative images of older people as dependent and incapable to overshadow the importance of empowering people with learning disabilities, and that Doris's quality of life had suffered as a result.

Disability

The traditional model of disability owes much to medical thinking. It is as if disability were a form of illness. Oliver and Sapey (1999) regard this medical perspective on disability to be part of what they call the 'individual model':

The individual model sees the problems that disabled people experience as being a direct consequence of their impairment. The major task of the professional is therefore to adjust the individual to the particular disabling condition. There are two aspects to this: first there is physical adjustment through rehabilitation programmes designed to return the individual to as near normal a state as possible; and, second there is psychological adjustment which helps the individual to come to terms with the physical limitations. (p. 13)

Superficially, this sounds reasonable enough, but once we start to delve more deeply, we begin to see how problematic it is. The main problem is that it is based on the assumption that the disability (that is, what *disables* a person) arises purely from their physical impairment. This is problematic because it fails to take account of the social context of disability – it fails to recognise that it is generally the social attitudes, the environmental barriers and the discriminatory assumptions and stereotypes that have more of a disabling effect than the impairment itself.

This is what is known as the social model of disability. It is so called because it emphasises the problems of focusing too narrowly on disabled people as individuals without taking into account the wider social context that can be very influential in shaping how disability is experienced.

When it comes to working with disabled people in a community care context, it is therefore important to make sure that we do not reinforce an individualistic model by failing to take account of social issues and the discrimination disabled people face because of:

- *Marginalisation and exclusion.* A tendency to fail to include disabled people – for example, not consulting them in matters that affect them (adopting a 'we know best' attitude).
- *Creating dependency.* Assuming that disabled equals 'not capable' can lead to too great an emphasis on service provision. The emphasis can easily become too narrowly focused on service provision, with inadequate attention paid to empowerment and independence.

In order to make sure that our community care practice is consistent with the principles of anti-disablist practice, we need at the very least to make sure that:

- We adopt a social rather than individual model of disability.
- We do not equate disability with incapacity – it can be a serious and costly mistake (in both human and financial terms) to focus unduly on negatives and problems and fail to take account of strengths and positives.
- We take all reasonable steps to focus on empowerment and avoiding dependency rather than falling into the trap of focusing too closely on care issues at the expense of a consideration of promoting independence.

> ### Exercise 3.4
>
> What images of disabled people are propagated by the media? How accurate do you feel they are? In what ways might such images and assumptions influence community care practice? How might you make sure that this does not cause any problems in terms of the quality of assessment and care offered? If you get the opportunity compare notes with one or more colleagues about these issues and see what you can learn from their perspectives.

Conclusion

For the sake of simplicity and clarity we have explored five separate areas of discrimination and considered how they relate to community care. However, there are two important points we need to emphasise. First, the five we have chosen are not the only ones. For example, we could have explored issues of discrimination relating to sexual identity or religion. Discrimination is a wide-ranging phenomenon and is not restricted to the examples we have given here.

Second, these forms of discrimination do not act in isolation. They interact and influence one another. Rather than separate entities, they are what Thompson (2001) calls 'dimensions of experience'. It is therefore important that we do not lose sight of the complex interactions of the various factors that contribute to discrimination. Part Three has been only a basic introduction to these important questions and should be seen as a gateway to the wider and more advanced writings on the subject.

> ### Practice Focus 3.6
>
> Keith was an advice worker who had been asked to work with David, a Chinese man with depression who had missed several appointments at his GP surgery. Keith arranged to see him, but David was very reluctant to talk and didn't turn up to any of the subsequent meetings that were arranged. Keith offered to visit him at home, but this offer was also refused. Keith, not realising the devastating effect that depression can have on motivation, decided that, if David didn't need help, then he wouldn't force it on him. He removed him from his referral list and thought no more about the matter.
>
> A few weeks later, while on a training course about cultural diversity, he became aware from a discussion with one of the other participants that there is often an expectation within Chinese culture in general that mental health issues should remain private and not be discussed outside of the immediate family. He was also made aware of how it feels to have to communicate in a language that is not the one you feel most comfortable with and realised that he had not asked David about language choice. On reflection, Keith wondered whether either of these points might explain David's reluctance to talk to him or accept help. Having been alerted

to how wider issues can impact on personal choice, he wondered about whether poverty might also be playing a part here. He discovered that it certainly was. David had not been able to work and had neither the money to travel to interviews nor suitable clothes for such occasions. Living in poor accommodation, he was ashamed to have someone like Keith visit him there, and he could not afford to travel to Keith's office when he was invited to. Keith had congratulated himself on acknowledging the discrimination that David was experiencing as a member of a minority community. However, it took him a while to realise that David was experiencing discrimination on the grounds of disability and class too. After discussing his learning with a colleague they realised that, not only was discrimination occurring in different and interconnected forms, but also at different levels. This was not just about Keith being discriminatory, but also about his employing organisation's practices being discriminatory too. They realised that, without translation facilities, the service offered to David by the advice centre was not as good as the service they could offer to callers whose first language was English. While claiming to be open to all it obviously wasn't in practice.

Undertaking community care work means working with people who are vulnerable and in need. Many, if not most, of them will be subject to one or more forms of discrimination. If we are not sensitive to, and aware of, the subtle and complex workings of discrimination, we can create problems rather than solve them. The lessons to be learned from Part Three, and from your further reading on the subject, are therefore very important indeed. We hope you will be able to draw upon what you have learned here in order to develop forms of practice that are emancipatory and empowering, based on principles of social justice, rather than forms of practice that risk adding insult to injury by reinforcing existing patterns of discrimination.

General background

Trevillion, S. and Beresford, P. (eds) (1996) *Meeting the Challenge: Social Work Education and the Community Care Revolution*, London, National Institute for Social Work.

These papers are themed around the education and training aspects of community care and have a strong focus on the involvement of service users.

Means, R. Morbey, H. and Smith, R. (2002) *From Community Care to Market Care? The Development of Welfare Services for Older People*, Bristol, The Policy Press.

Here the authors look at some of the policy issues that have underpinned the development of community care, both prior to and since the changes brought about by the NHS and Community Care Act 1990.

Blakemore, K. (1998) *Social Policy: An Introduction*, Buckingham, Open University Press.

There is a combination here of discussion around key concepts such as power and social control, and exploration of specific policy areas such as community care, housing and education.

Williams, F. (1989) *Social Policy: A Critical Introduction*, Cambridge, Polity Press.

As the title suggests, this book provides a critical overview of the main theoretical perspectives in welfare provision and examines their relationship with issues of class, race and gender. Although published some time ago now, it continues to be relevant and insightful.

Bytheway, B., Bacigalupo, V., Bornat, J., Johnson, J. and Spurr, S. (eds) (2002) *Understanding Care, Welfare and Community: A Reader*, London, Routledge.

This reader offers a very diverse mix of articles, written by academics, service users, carers and service providers. They are themed around issues of power, identity, rights and risks, and territories and boundaries. It provides food for thought about the 'taken-for-granted' nature of these well-used words and, as such, is a useful book for dipping into.

Care management

Challis, D., Chesterman, J., Luckett, R., Stewart, K. and Chessum, R. (2002) *Care Management in Social and Primary Health Care: The Gateshead Community Care Scheme*, Aldershot, Ashgate.

The Gateshead study was cited as an exemplar of intensive care management, and so this book offers interesting material regarding the maintenance of frail older people in the community. It highlights the interface between health and social care and explores a range of continuing concerns in this area.

Payne, M. (1995) *Social Work and Community Care*, Basingstoke, Palgrave Macmillan.

This book looks at the significant role that social workers play in community care and at what social work skills and values can bring to it. Payne explores the development of the concept, focuses on care planning and implementation and includes discussion of accountability.

Phillips, J. and Penhale, B. (eds) (1996) *Reviewing Care Management for Older People*, London, Jessica Kingsley.

This set of readings draws together a range of research findings on this subject and includes contributions on aspects such as multidisciplinary assessment, the needs of elders from ethnic minorities and care management with people who have dementia.

Systematic practice

Egan, G. (2002) *The Skilled Helper: A Problem-Management Approach to Helping*, 7th edn, California, Brooks/Cole Publishing.

A well-established textbook popular with a wide range of professional helpers. It provides a good discussion of issues relating to systematic practice.

Thompson, N. (2000) *Understanding Social Work: Preparing for Practice*, Basingstoke, Palgrave Macmillan.

Establishes the importance of adopting a systematic approach to practice.

Thompson, N. (2002) *People Skills*, 2nd edn, Basingstoke, Palgrave Macmillan.

Sets systematic practice in the overall context of skills of intervention in working with people and their problems in a wide variety of settings.

Empowerment

Adams, R. (2003) *Social Work and Empowerment*, 3rd edn, Basingstoke, Palgrave Macmillan.

This is a classic introductory text on the subject and integrates theoretical models and methods with practice, be it with individuals, groups or communities.

Humphries, B. (ed.) (1996) *Critical Perspectives on Empowerment*, Birmingham, Venture Press.

Creates food for thought about the dangers of oversimplifying empowerment.

Jack, R. (ed.) (1995) *Empowerment in Community Care*, London, Chapman Hall.

This edited collection looks at empowerment specifically within a community care context. As well as exploring issues around definition and rationale, it includes contributions which relate to a wide range of user groups, and a range of related issues, such as rights and peer support.

Braye, S. and Preston-Shoot, M. (1995) *Empowering Practice in Social Care*, Buckingham, Open University Press.

This is a useful text in relation to social care in general and, more particularly, in terms of underpinning values and conflicts of interest.

Thursz, D., Nusberg, C. and Prather, J. (eds) (1995) *Empowering Older People: An International Approach*, London, Cassell.

This is a thought-provoking set of readings from a wide range of countries including Mexico, Pakistan and Japan. It focuses on empowering organisations as well as individuals.

Risk management

Thompson, N. and Thompson, S. (2002) *Understanding Social Care: A Guide to the Underpinning Knowledge Requirements of S/NVQ Awards in Care at Level 4*, Lyme Regis, Russell House Publishing.

This guide for practitioners studying for NVQ Level 4 in Care contains a short section on risk assessment, which provides a good starting point on which to build.

Parsloe, P. (ed.) (1999) *Risk Assessment in Social Care and Social Work*, London, Jessica Kingsley.

This collection has contributions from academics and practitioners, and covers broad issues such as ethics and accountability as well as focusing on specific areas such as the management of risk in mental health work.

Kemshall, H. and Pritchard, J. (eds) (1996) *Good Practice in Risk Assessment and Risk Management*, London, Jessica Kingsley.

This also covers a wide range of practice situations and social care settings. While it has a strong focus on practice, it emphasises the need to locate practice in a knowledge base.

Langan, J. and Lindow, V. (2004) *Living with Risk*, Bristol, The Policy Press.

A report which focuses on risk assessment and management with people returning to the community from psychiatric hospitals. It explores the issues from a number of perspectives, particularly that of service users.

Reflective practice

Schön, D.A. (1983) *The Reflective Practitioner: How Professionals Think in Action*, New York, Basic Books.

A classic, ground-breaking text on the subject.

Thompson, N. (2000) *Theory and Practice in Human Services*, 2nd edn, Buckingham, Open University Press.

Sets reflective practice in the context of the relationship between theory and practice.

Gould, M. and Taylor, I. (eds) (1995) *Reflective Learning for Social Work*, Aldershot, Arena.

A collection which brings together discussions on reflective learning, from both practice and academic settings.

Yelloly, M. and Henkel, M. (eds) (1995) *Learning and Teaching in Social Work: Towards Reflective Practice*, London, Jessica Kingsley.

A number of contemporary issues in professional education are debated here, including models of professionalism and multidisciplinary training.

Evidence-based practice

Sheldon, B. and Chilvers, R. (2000) *Evidence-Based Social Care: A Study of Prospects and Problems*, Lyme Regis, Russell House Publishing.

Based on a large-scale survey focusing on, amongst other issues, how services can be evaluated more effectively, this study identifies obstacles to progress but also moves on to offer ways forward.

Webb, S. A. (2001) 'Some Considerations of the Validity of Evidence-Based Practice in Social Work' *British Journal of Social Work* 31(5).

A critical commentary of evidence-based practice. Webb questions some of the assumptions of the approach.

Roberts, R.A. and Yeager, K.R. (eds) (2004) *Evidence-based Practice Manual*, Oxford, Oxford University Press.

A massive compendium (over 1,000 pages) of essays relating to evidence-based practice.

The legal basis of community care

Bateman, N. (2003) *Welfare Rights*, London, Care and Health Ltd.

In addition to sections on particular welfare benefits, this book contains a useful section on tactics in welfare rights work and a succinct overview of the benefits system.

Brayne, H. and Broadbent, G. (2002) *Legal Materials for Social Workers*, Oxford, Oxford University Press.

This book has a wide range, but devotes a section to community care issues in particular. In its introductory section the authors also refer to human rights and anti-discrimination legislation.

Wadham, J. and Mountfield, H. (1999) *Blackstone's Guide to the Human Rights Act 1998*, London, Blackstone Press Ltd.

Contains a copy of the Act itself and provides a short introduction which helps place this landmark legislation in its context.

Watson, J. and Woolf, M. (2003) *Human Rights Act Toolkit*, London, LAG Education and Service Trust Ltd.

As the title suggests, this is a more practical guide which is designed to help public and voluntary sector workers to understand the Act and the duties it places on them.

Developments in law and policy

Clements, L. and Read, J. (2003) *Disabled People and European Human Rights*, Bristol, The Policy Press.

Provides an overview of key policy and legislative changes in terms of human rights and looks at the implications for disabled people. The final chapter advocates for the Human Rights Act 1998 to be used to the benefit of disabled people and offers guidance to that end.

Department of Health (2001) *National Service Framework for Older People*, London, DoH.

This government document sets out a programme of reform which aims to address inequity in care provision and help ensure that standards in health and social care provision to older people are improved.

Gilbert, P. (2003) *The Value of Everything: Social Work and its Importance in the Field of Mental Health*, Lyme Regis, Russell House Publishing.

Chapter 3 provides a good discussion of changes in law and policy in relation to mental health.

Rideout, P. (2003) *Care Standards: A Practical Guide*, Bristol, Jordan Publishing.

This comprehensive guide is a useful source of information in respect of recent changes in the regulation of residential care for vulnerable adults.

(E)quality assurance

Adams, R. (1998) *Quality Social Work*, Basingstoke, Palgrave Macmillan.

A thought-provoking discussion of varying approaches to ensuring quality in social work.

Thompson, N. (2001) *Anti-Discriminatory Practice*, 3rd edn, Basingstoke, Palgrave Macmillan.

A classic text which explains discrimination in terms of three levels: personal, cultural and structural.

Thompson, N. (2003) *Promoting Equality: Challenging Discrimination and Oppression*, 2nd edn, Basingstoke, Palgrave Macmillan.

A follow-up to *Anti-Discriminatory Practice* which explores the issues in more depth.

Thompson, S. (2002) *From Where I'm Sitting*, Lyme Regis, Russell House Publishing.

This training manual urges people working in the field of social care with older people to take a step back and consider how that caregiving is perceived from the service users' viewpoint.

Partnership

Harrison, R., Mann, G., Murphy, M., Taylor, A. and Thompson, N. (2003) *Partnership Made Painless*, Lyme Regis, Russell House Publishing.

A useful introduction to macro-level partnership working – that is, collaborations at the organisational level, but also has a number of implications for micro-level partnership working.

Thompson, N. (2002) *Building the Future: Social Work with Children, Young People and Their Families*, Lyme Regis, Russell House Publishing.

Discusses partnership working in a child care context but much of it can be readily translated into a community care context.

Thompson, N. and Thompson, S. (2002) *Understanding Social Care: A Guide to the Underpinning Knowledge Requirements of S/NVQ Awards in Care at Level 4*, Lyme Regis, Russell House Publishing.

Provides a basic introduction to the idea of partnership in social care.

Sullivan, H. and Skelcher, C. (2002) *Working Across Boundaries: Collaboration in Public Services*, Basingstoke, Palgrave Macmillan.

An interesting analysis of the phenomenon of partnership in public service planning and delivery.

Payne, M. (2000) *Teamwork in Multiprofessional Care*, Basingstoke, Palgrave Macmillan.

Offers a useful discussion of teamwork in a multidisciplinary context.

Relevant websites

www.bgop.org.uk

This site outlines the main tenets of The Better Government for Older People Initiative and includes issues such as promoting independence, community regeneration and race and age diversity.

www.communitycare.co.uk

Website of *Community Care* magazine and a good source of information.

www.careandhealth.co.uk

Another useful magazine website.

www.wales.gov.uk

Website of the National Assembly for Wales – contains a lot of relevant material (see also *www.doh.gov.uk* for UK-wide materials)

www.gscc.org.uk

This is the General Social Care Council site. It has links with the relevant regulatory bodies in Wales, Scotland and Northern Ireland.

www.open.gov.uk

This site gives access to over 1,000 government websites and to a wide variety of government publications.

www.elsc.org.uk

The 'Electronic Library for Social Care' – a very effective gateway into a number of relevant sites.

www.york.ac.uk/inst/spru

As its title suggests, The Social Policy Research Unit has a strong focus on research into, and evaluation of, welfare services.

www.sosig.ac.uk

A broad-based social science site with relevant links.

www.ncil.org.uk

The National Centre for Independent Living's website. It has a notice board feature which tracks current debates in this field.

www.disabilitynow.org.uk

The website for *Disability Now*, a campaigning newspaper.

www.be-evidence-based.com

Highlights useful research material, including that on the involvement of service users.

Conclusion

Community care is a huge topic. Much has already been written about it and no doubt much more will continue to be written about it. It has not been possible for us to provide a comprehensive account of the subject and it would have been foolish to try in such a short space. The aim of the *Theory into Practice* series is to provide clear overviews of particular areas of thought, link them to practice, explore the implications in terms of discrimination and oppression and provide a gateway to the wider and more in-depth literature. We hope you will agree that that is precisely what we have achieved here.

Inevitably what we have presented here will reflect our own backgrounds, interests and priorities. It will present a picture of community care as we see it, which is not necessarily the way other people will see it. However, we hope that we will have provided enough food for thought to stimulate a great deal of debate, discussion and further study so that you can go on to broaden and deepen your understanding and make important links with practice.

Community care is important. It is a topic close to our hearts. We hope that, in our modest efforts here, we will have played a part in helping other people to recognise it as important and to take it to their hearts. Community care is *not* a bureaucratic, mechanised rationing of resources (although there are clear and strong pressures to take it in that direction). It is a scheme whereby a mature democracy seeks to ensure, as far as possible, that its most vulnerable citizens receive the help and support they need when they need it. That help and support should be on offer without its recipients having to sacrifice their dignity, independence, self-esteem or self-respect.

The community care system is not perfect – far from it. However, committed workers can make a positive contribution to building on its strengths and positives and doing whatever they reasonably can – individually and collectively – to identify and counteract its shortcomings. It is a major challenge, but we hope you will be motivated to support one another in rising to it and we wish you well in doing so.

References

Acheson, D. (1998) *Independent Inquiry into 'Health Inequalities' Report*, London, The Stationery Office.

Adams, R. (1998) *Quality Social Work*, Basingstoke, Macmillan – now Palgrave Macmillan.

Adams, R. (2002) 'Quality Assurance', in Adams *et al.* (2002).

Adams, R., Dominelli, L. and Payne, M. (eds) (2002) *Critical Practice in Social Work*, Basingstoke, Palgrave Macmillan.

Ahmad, W.I.U. and Atkin, K. (1996a) ' "Race" and Community Care: An Introduction', in Ahmad and Atkin (1996b).

Ahmad, W.I.U. and Atkin, K. (eds) (1996b) *'Race' and Community Care*, Buckingham, Open University Press.

Bagilhole, B. (1997) *Equal Opportunities and Social Policy: Issues of Gender, Race and Disability*, Harlow, Longman.

Baxter, C. (ed.) (2001) *Managing Diversity and Inequality in Health Care*, Edinburgh, Baillière Tindall.

Baxter C. and Toon, P. 'Nurses, Doctors and the Meaning of Holism: Interprofessionalism and Values in Primary Care' in Baxter 2001.

Beresford, P. (2001) 'Where Do You Stand with Service Users?' *Journal of Social Work*, 1(1).

Blair, T. (1996) Speech to Labour Party conference.

Blair, T. (1998) *The Third Way: New Politics for the New Century*, Fabian Pamphlet 588, London, The Fabian Society.

Blair, T. (1999) Speech on moral standards, *The Guardian*, 6th September.

Blakemore, K. (1998) *Social Policy: An Introduction*, Buckingham, Open University Press.

Braye, S. and Preston-Shoot, M. (1995) *Empowering Practice in Social Care*, Buckingham, Open University Press.

Brechin, A., Brown, H. and Eby, M.A. (eds) (2000) *Critical Practice in Health and Social Care*, London, Sage.

Bytheway, B., Bacigalupo, V., Bornat, J., Johnson, J. and Spurr, S. (eds) (2002) *Understanding Care, Welfare and Community*, London, Routledge.

Caldock, K. and Nolan, M. (1994) 'Assessment and Community Care: Are the Reforms Working?', *Generations Review*, 4(4).

Carter, T. and Beresford, P. (2000) *Age and Change: Models of Involvement for Older People*, York, York Press.

Centre for Policy on Ageing (1990) *Community Life: A Code of Practice for Community Care*, London, Centre for Policy on Ageing.

Chiu, L. F. (2001) 'Extending the Team Outwards: Building Partnerships and Teamworks with Communities' in Baxter (2001).

Clements, L. (2002) 'Community Care Law and the Human Rights Act 1998', in Bytheway et al. (2002).

Coleman, P.G., McKiernan, F., Mills, M. and Speck, P. (2002) 'Spiritual Belief and Quality of Life: The Experience of Older Bereaved Spouses', *Quality in Ageing*, 3(1).

Crompton, I. and Thompson, N. (2000) *The Human Rights Act 1998: A Training Resource Pack*, Wrexham, Learning Curve Publishing.

Dale, B. (1999) *Managing Quality*, 3rd edn, Oxford, Blackwell.

Dalrymple, J. and Burke, B. (1995) *Anti-Oppressive Practice, Social Care and the Law*,

Davies, C. (2000) 'Frameworks for Regulation and Accountability: Threat or Opportunity?' in Brechin et al. (2000).

Davies, M. (ed.) (2002) *The Blackwell Companion to Social Work*, 2nd edn, Oxford, Blackwell.

Davis C. (2000) Vive la Difference: That's What will Make Collaboration Work', *Nursing Times* 96 (15):27

Department of Health (1991a) *Care Management and Assessment: Managers' Guide*, London, HMSO.

Department of Health (1991b) *Care Management and Assessment: Practitioners' Guide*, London, HMSO.

Department of Health (1999) *Better Care, Higher Standards: A Charter for Long-Term Care*, London, HMSO.

Department of Health (1999) *No Secrets: Guidance on Developing and Implementing Multi-Agency Policies and Procedures to Protect Vulnerable Adults from Abuse*, London, HMSO.

Department of Health (1999) *Social Services in 1998–1999: The Personal Social Services Performance Assessment Framework*, London, HMSO.

Department of Health (2001) *National Service Framework for Older People*, London, HMSO.

Ellison, N. and Pierson, J. (eds) (1998) *Developments in British Social Policy*, Basingstoke, Macmillan – now Palgrave Macmillan.

Faulkes, D. (1995) *Administrative Law*, 8th edn, London, Butterworth.

Finch, J. and Groves, D. (1983) (eds) *A Labour of Love: Women, Work and Caring,* London, Routledge and Kegan Paul.

Fook, J. (2002) *Social Work: Critical Theory and Practice*, London, Sage.

George, V. and Page, R. (eds) (1995) *Modern Thinkers on Welfare*, London, Prentice-Hall.

Glasby, J. and Littlechild, R. (2002) *Social Work and Direct Payments*, Bristol, The Policy Press.

Gorman, H. and Postle, K. (2003) *Transforming Community Care: A Distorted Vision?* Birmingham, Venture Press.

Gould, N. and Taylor, I. (eds) (1996) *Reflective Learning for Social Work*, Aldershot, Arena.

Guirdham, M. (1999) *Communicating Across Cultures,* Basingstoke, Palgrave Macmillan.

Hill, H. (2001) *Blackstone's Guide to the Race Relations (Amendment) Act 2000*, Oxford, Oxford University Press.

Hoyes, L., Lart, R., Means, R. and Taylor, M. (1994) *Community Care in Transition*, York, Joseph Rowntree Foundation.

Hughes, G. (ed.) (1998) *Imagining Welfare Futures*, London, Routledge.

Humphries, B. (1996) *Critical Perspectives in Empowerment*, Birmingham, Venture Press.

Jack, R. (ed.) (1995) *Empowerment in Community Care*, London, Chapman and Hall.

✳ James, J. and Baxter, C. (2001) 'The Multiracial Team: The Challenges Ahead', in Baxter (2001).

Jones, C. (2001) 'Voices From the Front Line: State Social Workers and New Labour', *British Journal of Social Work*, 31(4).

Jones, C. and Novak, T. (1999) *Poverty, Welfare and the Disciplinary State*, London, Routledge.

Jordan, B. (1990) *Social Work in an Unjust Society*, Hemel Hempstead, Harvester Wheatsheaf.

Jordan, B. (2000) 'Conclusion: Tough Love: Social Work Practice in UK Society', in Stepney and Ford (2000).

Kemshall, H. and Pritchard, J. (eds) (1996) *Good Practice in Risk Assessment and Risk Management*, London, Jessica Kingsley.

Lavatte, M. and Pratt, A. (1997) *Social Policy: A Conceptual and Theoretical Framework*, London, Sage.

Lesnik, B. (ed.) (1997) *Change in Social Work*, Aldershot, Ashgate.

Lewis, G. (2000) *Rethinking Social Policy*, Buckingham, Open University Press.

Lewis, G., Gerwirtz, S. and Clarke, J. (2000) *Rethinking Social Policy*, London, Sage.

MacDonald, C. and Myers, F. (1995) *Assessment and Care Management: The Practitioner Speaks*, Stirling, University of Stirling.

Macdonald, G. (2002) 'The Evidence-Based Perspective', in Davies (2002).

Mandelstam, M. (1999) *Community Care Practice and the Law*, 2nd edn, Cromwell Press.

Means, R., Morbey, H. and Smith, R. (2002) *From Community Care to Market Care? The Development of Welfare Services for Older People*, Bristol, The Policy Press.

Means, R., Richards, S. and Smith, R. (2003) *Community Care: Policy and Practice*, 3rd edn, Basingstoke, Palgrave Macmillan.

Midwinter, E. (1990) 'An Ageing World', *Ageing and Society* 10.

Morrison, T. (2001) *Supervision in Social Care: An Action Learning Approach*, 2nd edn, Brighton, Pavilion.

National Assembly for Wales/University of Wales, Bangor (2000) *Moving On: A Report on the Lost in Care Conference*, Bangor, University of Wales Bangor in association with the National Assembly for Wales.

Nicholson, K. and Randall, H. (1999) *A Guide to the Local Government Act 1999*, London, Butterworth.

Oliver, M. and Sapey, B. (1999) *Social Work with Disabled People*, 2nd edn, Basingstoke, Macmillan.

Orme, J. and Glastonbury, B. (1993) *Care Management: Tasks and Workloads*, Basingstoke, Macmillan – now Palgrave Macmillan.

Parsloe, P. (ed.) (1999) *Risk Assessment in Social Care and Social Work*, London, Jessica Kingsley.

Peace, S., Kellaher, L. and Willcocks, D. (1997) *Re-evaluating Residential Care*, Buckingham, Open University Press.

Petch, A., Stalker, K., Taylor, C. and Taylor, J. (1994) *Assessment and Care Management Pilot Projects in Scotland: An Overview*, Stirling, University of Stirling.

Phillips, J. and Penhale, B. (eds) (1996) *Reviewing Care Management for Older People*, London, Jessica Kingsley.

Phillips, J. (1996) 'Reviewing the Literature on Care Management', in Phillips and Penhale (1996).

Postle, K. (2002) 'Working "Between the Idea and the Reality": Ambiguities and Tensions in Care Managers' Work', *British Journal of Social Work*, 32(3).

Powell, M., Exworthy, M. and Berney, L. (2001) 'Playing the Game of Partnership, in Sykes *et al.* (2001).

Powell, M. and Hewitt, M. (2002) *Welfare State and Welfare Change*, Buckingham, Open University Press.

Ramcharan, P. (1997) *Empowerment in Everyday Life: Learning Disability*, London, Jessica Kingsley.

Rawaf, S. and Powell, K. (2001) 'Clinical Governance', in Baxter (2001).

Roberts, G., Griffiths, A., James, S., Owen, G. and Williams, H. (1998) *Gofal: Community Care in Wales (A Training and Resource Pack)*, Cardiff, CCETSW.

Rogers, C. (1961) *Client Centred Therapy: Its Current Practice, Theory and Implications*, London, Constable.

Schön, D.A. (1983) *The Reflective Practitioner: How Professionals Think in Action*, New York, Basic Books.

Schön, D.A. (1987) *Educating the Reflective Practitioner*, San Francisco, CA, Jossey Bass.

Schön, D.A. (1992) 'The Crisis of Professional Knowledge and the Pursuit of an Epistemology of Practice', *Journal of Interprofessional Care*, 6(1).

Seed, P. and Kaye, G. (1994) *Handbook for Assessing and Managing Care in the Community*, London, Jessica Kingsley.

Servian, R. (1996) *Theorising Empowerment: Individual Power and Community Care*, Bristol, The Policy Press.

Shaw, I. F. (1996) *Evaluating in Practice*, Aldershot, Arena.

Sheldon, B. (2001) 'The Validity of Evidence-based Practice in Social Work: A Reply to Stephen Webb', *British Journal of Social Work*, 31(5).

Sheldon, B. and Chilvers, R. (2000) *Evidence-Based Social Care: A Study of Prospects and Problems*, Lyme Regis, Russell House Publishing.

Smale, G., Tuson, G., with Biehal, N. and Marsh, P. (1993) *Empowerment, Assessment, Care Management and the Skilled Worker*, London, HMSO.

Stepney, P. and Ford, D. (eds) (2000) *Social Work Models, Methods and Theories*, Lyme Regis, Russell House Publishing.

Sullivan, H. and Skelcher, C. (2002) *Working Across Boundaries: Collaboration in Public Services,* Basingstoke, Palgrave Macmillan.

Sykes, R., Bochel, C. and Ellison, N. (eds) (2001) *Social Policy Review 13: Developments and Debates: 2000–2001*, Bristol, The Policy Press.

Thompson, J. and Matthias, P. (eds) (1998) *Standards and Learning Disability,* London, Balliere Tindall.

Thompson, N. (1995) *Age and Dignity: Working With Older People*, Aldershot, Arena.

Thompson, N. (1999) *Stress Matters*, Birmingham, Pepar.

Thompson, N. (2000a) *Understanding Social Work: Preparing for Practice*, Basingstoke, Palgrave Macmillan.

Thompson, N. (2000b) 'Towards A New Professionalism', in National Assembly for Wales/University of Wales, Bangor (2000).

Thompson, N. (2000b) *Theory and Practice in Human Services*, 2nd edn, Buckingham, Open University Press.

Thompson, N. (2001) *Anti-Discriminatory Practice*, 3rd edn, Basingstoke, Palgrave Macmillan.

Thompson, N. (2002a) *People Skills*, 2nd edn, Basingstoke, Palgrave Macmillan.

Thompson, N. (2002b) *Building the Future: Social Work with Children, Young People and Their Families*, Lyme Regis, Russell House Publishing.

Thompson, N. (ed.) (2002c) *Loss and Grief: A Guide for Human Services Practitioners*, Basingstoke, Palgrave Macmillan.

Thompson, N. (2003a) *Promoting Equality: Challenging Discrimination and Oppression*, Basingstoke, 2nd edn, Palgrave Macmillan.

Thompson, N. (2003b) *Communication and Language: A Handbook of Theory and Practice*, Basingstoke, Palgrave Macmillan.

Thompson, N. and Bates, J. (1998) *Learning from Other Disciplines: Lessons from Management Theory and Nurse Education*, Norwich, University of East Anglia Social Work Monographs.

Thompson, N. and Thompson, S. (2001) 'Empowering Older People: Beyond the Care Model', *Journal of Social Work*, 1(1).

Thompson, N. and Thompson, S. (2002) *Understanding Social Care: A Guide to the Underpinning Knowledge Requirements of the S/NVQ Level 4 Awards in Care*, Lyme Regis, Russell House Publishing.

Thompson, N. Osada, M. and Anderson, B. (1994) *Practice Teaching in Social Work: A Handbook*, 2nd edn, Birmingham, Pepar.

Thompson, N., Murphy, M. and Stradling, S. (1996) *Meeting the Stress Challenge*, Lyme Regis, Russell House Publishing.

Thompson, N., Murphy, M. and Stradling, S. (1997) 'Stress and the Organizational Context of Change' in Lesnik (1997).

Thompson, S. (2002a) *From Where I'm Sitting*, Lyme Regis, Russell House Publishing.

Thompson, S. (2002b) 'Old Age', in Thompson (2002c).

Thursz, D., Nusberg, C. and Prather, J. (1995) *Empowering Older People: An International Approach*, London, Cassell.

Trevillion, S. and Beresford, P. (eds) (1996) *Meeting the Challenge: Social Work Education and the Community Care Revolution*, London, National Institute for Social Work.

Wadham, J. (1999) *Blackstone's Guide to the Human Rights Act 1998*, Oxford, Blackstone.

Wadham, J. and Mountfield, H. (1999) *Blackstone's Guide to the Human Rights Act 1998*, London, Blackstone Press Ltd.

Waterhouse, R. (2000) *Lost in Care,* London, The Stationery Office.

Webb, S. A. (2001) 'Some Considerations of the Validity of Evidence-based Practice in Social Work', *British Journal of Social Work*, 31(1).

Weinstein, J. (1998) 'The Professions and Their Inter-relationships' in Thompson and Matthias (1998).

Williams, F. (1989) *Social Policy: A Critical Introduction*, Cambridge, Polity Press.

Yelloly, M. and Henkel, M. (eds) (1995) *Learning and Teaching in Social Work: Towards Reflective Practice*, London, Jessica Kingsley.

Index